Over-Tested and Under-Prepared

D1414067

The curriculum-driven instructional model has been the standard method of teaching for more than a century, but it is consistently failing to produce well-educated citizens and lifelong learners. Pressured by standardized testing and rigid pacing guidelines, teachers are forced to cover too much content too quickly, without being able to meet the needs of individual students. In this powerful new book from acclaimed author and speaker Bob Sornson, you'll learn how shifting from curriculum-based instruction to competency based learning can help students become more successful, confident, and engaged learners. Topics include:

♦ Understanding the curriculum-driven model and the problems with "cover and sort" methodology;
♦ Making the transition from curriculum-driven to competency based learning;
♦ Identifying crucial learning outcomes and giving students all the time and instruction needed to fully master these outcomes;
♦ Building a positive teaching and learning environment;
♦ And more!

Each chapter is short and easy to digest, and provides compelling research, strategies, and anecdotes to inspire conversation and action. Teachers, administrators, and community leaders will all find helpful resources and arguments for re-working our current educational system into a new, dynamic model of teaching and learning.

Bob Sornson is the founder of the Early Learning Foundation and is a former classroom teacher and school administrator. He works with schools and education organizations across the country, focusing primarily on developing comprehensive programs that support early learning success.

Over-Tested and Under-Prepared

Using Competency Based Learning to Transform Our Schools

Bob Sornson

Routledge
Taylor & Francis Group

NEW YORK AND LONDON

First published 2016
by Routledge
711 Third Avenue, New York, NY 10017

and by Routledge
2 Park Square, Milton Park, Abingdon, Oxon, OX14 4RN

*Routledge is an imprint of the Taylor & Francis Group,
an informa business*

Library of Congress Cataloging-in-Publication Data
A catalog record for this book has been requested

ISBN: 978-1-138-95680-3 (hbk)
ISBN: 978-1-138-95681-0 (pbk)
ISBN: 978-1-315-66553-5 (ebk)

Typeset in Palatino
by Apex CoVantage, LLC

Printed and bound in the United States of America by Publishers Graphics,
LLC on sustainably sourced paper.

To every educator who knows there is a better way and who holds on to the belief that somehow adults can thoughtfully consider, collaborate, and find that way.

To every parent who believes that children can fall in love with learning and wants each child to have an opportunity to find success.

To every child who loves to learn.

Contents

About the Author

Bob Sornson is an education leader calling for programs and practices that support competency based learning, early learning success, and high-quality early childhood learning programs. He is the father of four grown children and works internationally with school districts, universities, and parent organizations.

Courtesy of Lynn Gregg

Born and raised in Detroit, MI, along with his six siblings, Bob earned a bachelor's and master's degree at the University of Michigan, an education specialist degree from Central Michigan University, and his Ph.D. from Andrews University. For over thirty years, he worked as a teacher and as an administrator in Michigan public schools, developed an acclaimed model early learning success initiative, and in 2001 founded the **Early Learning Foundation**.

A prolific author, Bob has written best-selling books for educators, parents, and children, along with many journal publications. His books include *Essential Math Skills* (Shell Education), *Fanatically Formative* (Corwin Press), *Stand in My Shoes: Kids Learning about Empathy* (Love and Logic Press), *The Juice Box Bully* (Early Learning Foundation Press), *Teaching and Joy* (ASCD), and *Creating Classrooms Where Teachers Love to Teach and Students Love to Learn* (Love and Logic Press). He has offered workshops and keynotes in forty-seven states and in other nations.

Bob Sornson is dedicated to giving far more students a real chance for success. Schools that cover, test, and sort do not effectively serve the needs of kids, families, or society. Nor do schools that allow students to fall into patterns of struggle and failure in the early years of learning. Nor do parents who do not yet know how to build positive family routines, set limits without anger, and help build the solid base of connection and love that allow children to thrive and build purposeful lives. In modern society, we are challenged to use the wealth of knowledge and information available to us to build systems and societies in which kids thrive, care for each other, demonstrate personal character, love to learn, and work collaboratively.

Bob's work involves developing thought patterns, behavior patterns, and institutional patterns to build a world we are proud to bequeath to our children and grandchildren. He lives with his wife Nancy in Brighton, MI, and can be contacted at earlylearningfoundation.com.

Acknowledgments

After more than three decades of "school reform," the disappointing implementation and results of No Child Left Behind, and the thinly disguised federalization of schools that was Race to the Top, the American public has become disheartened. They question whether education leaders and our government have the capacity to thoughtfully consider and implement a plan for the meaningful improvement of our system of education. Many educators are discouraged. Principals and teachers wonder where the joy went. Young men and women with the capacity to be extraordinary teachers look for another path.

And yet, everywhere I travel there are educators, parents, and community leaders who still have that spark in their eyes, holding on to a vision of learning systems that effectively serve students of every race and level of affluence, giving our children a chance to compete in the global society, inspiring a love of learning that can last a lifetime. This book is for you.

> The ultimate measure of a man is not where he stands in moments of comfort and convenience, but where he stands at times of challenge and controversy.
> —Martin Luther King, Jr.

To my great fortune, I get to meet and work with people who believe in their hearts and souls that we can build educational systems and institutions that truly serve our students, respecting their differences and honoring their strengths. They are not deterred from effective action by political drama and smothering bureaucracies. They are committed to building a better world for our children, and schools that work is part of that vision. They are found from Mississippi to Michigan, from

California to Maine, and in nations around the world. They inspire me.

I am especially grateful to the following people who made this book possible:

To Lauren Davis, my editor at Routledge, who from the first day she received my book proposal understood the message and believed there is an audience, and whose enthusiasm for this work moved it forward with astonishing positive energy.

To my amazing colleagues, whose insights helped shape this book. Thank you, Peggy Voigt, Derek Wheaton, Shannon Samulski, Chris Sturgis, Jim Tucker, Debbie Davis, Debbie Krauss, Lisa Scott, Tom Searcy, and Patty Steele.

To Casey Reason and Jim Scott, who share my tribulations and never ever advise me to play it safe.

To Rebecca, Matt, Alicia, and Molly, whose lives inspire my belief that ideas can make a difference and that I might find a way to shine a light.

To Nancy, who walks the path with me, whose kindness and decency surrounds every project and each day.

Reader's Guide

This book describes a model of learning unlike the one most of us experienced as students. It is my hope that readers will respond to the clear need for improved systems and refrain from the ever handy "We can't possibly do that because it has not been done like that before" response. Instead, imagine the creation of a new way, based on solid science and a heavy dose of common sense.

The first chapters begin with a look at what's possible, just enough to fill your heart with hope. Then we look back at the intended design of the education model we've used in schools for well more than a hundred years, with an eye for understanding why it was built as it is. By understanding the basic architecture of our system, we can more fully understand why it no longer serves the vast majority of students who desperately need an opportunity to become successful learners. Chapters nine through seventeen describe a new way of thinking about learning, in school and in life. Subsequent chapters describe the many ongoing efforts to build and use competency based learning systems. In the final chapters, we consider the steps you might take to lead the transformation in your school or community.

Educators, parents, students, and community leaders can study this text with many varied purposes, perhaps including the following:

♦ Read and share. Create a new vision for schools and learning that better serves students, parents, communities, and employers. Become an idea leader in your community.
♦ Read with the purpose of gathering resources or specific ideas for the transformation you already want to occur.
♦ Create personal or professional learning communities, using this book as a catalyst to dialog and collaboration toward the creation of new learning systems.

- Identify crucial learning outcomes for yourself or your organization, and use the many resources in this book to help you design a plan for sustained learning.
- Develop a leadership team to transform your schools or to build synergy between learning organizations, and build your transformation plan with the insights of those who have already traveled this path.

> You have brains in your head. You have feet in your shoes. You can steer yourself any direction you choose.
>
> —Dr. Seuss

Introduction

With only a month remaining in the school year, a young high school biology teacher is confronted with an unpleasant challenge. Three more chapters to go. He's teaching an honors class, but for the past several months he's been struggling to manage behavior and keep his students on-task. Many of them are frustrated and struggling to understand the material. Some have already disengaged from the learning process, having decided that science is too hard, not fun, and incredibly boring.

Three more chapters, with content including Population Ecology, Behavioral Biology, Community Biology, Ecosystems, and Conservation Biology. All the other Bio teachers are on-track to finish every chapter in the text, and the district clearly expects him to cover all this content. So he will rush through instruction for the science concepts he loves with students who are already disinterested or disconnected.

Half-way through the year, a third grade teacher prepares to move on to the next math lesson. She's been teaching for many years, but it is getting harder. The pressure of the state assessment looms. Looking around her classroom, she can easily identify which students love math. There are only a few. The others don't get it. The math program moves so quickly through the material. It feels like a race.

Her district has adopted a math program that allows no room for variance. Everyone gets the same lesson on the same day. Some of the kids lack basic number sense. Many of them have memorized facts and formulas but do not fully comprehend why these rules apply. Spiraling, they told her. Don't slow down. In a few months the expertly designed math curriculum will spiral around and cover the same material, so if students don't understand basic concepts now, just keep going. Teaching math used to be fun, but not anymore.

It's the beginning of the year. A sixth grade teacher considers her new class, goofy adolescents vying for attention and respect, searching for social connection, hoping for safety and status. But in her hands is the pacing guide, the guide for what must be taught, how quickly, and in what sequence.

She looks at her beautiful students. Every impulse in her begs to get to know them, build relationships with them. She wants to build a positive classroom culture, help them get to know each other, set standards for how we treat others and want to be treated. She would like to assess their learning needs and figure out each child's strengths. She would like to find out their special interests, the things that might motivate them to work a little harder. But she cannot.

In response to diminished outcomes on the state test, her district has adopted a more rigorous curriculum, a pacing guide for every subject, and biweekly assessments. Each day she is required to write the code for the CCSS standards that are being addressed by today's lessons on the whiteboard. If an administrator comes into the classroom and finds that she is not focused on those standards, she could be reprimanded.

Scanning her classroom, she sees the students who are nervous and socially awkward. She pauses, makes eye contact with each of them, and smiles. She notices the kids who are wiggly, who need movement and lots of practice learning to be calm and self-regulated. Then glancing at the pacing guide, she forges ahead. Ready or not, here it comes.

In the 21st century, good teachers are being asked to use the supercharged version of a curriculum-driven instructional model that treats kids as if they were learning on an assembly line. Covering way too much content at an unreasonable rate, with rigid pacing guides that make it impossible to find time to shape instruction to meet the individual needs of students, the system is breaking down. In spite of teaching to the test, our children are not doing better on international comparisons or compared to previous decades. Good teachers are discouraged. Many of the best and brightest college students cannot imagine subjecting themselves to working in such a broken system. State and national legislators fiddle mindlessly with our schools,

adding layers of regulation that confuse and befuddle both educators and parents. In the information age, an era in which
learning skills and the desire to learn have never been more
important, many capable students are not developing the skills
needed to achieve economic and personal success.

In this book, we will explore simple ideas that will help
teacher-leaders, administrators, and parents create learning systems in which both educators and students have a much better
chance to succeed. The steps are simple. Identify crucial learning
outcomes. Teach and practice crucial learning outcomes for as
long as it takes to develop competency. Design instruction for
crucial outcomes in a student's zone of proximal development.
Learn to track the progress of each student along the pathways
to crucial outcomes. Include students in the planning process
for developing advanced-level learning plans. Deliver instruction
and monitor progress in all the domains of development that
contribute to a life of learning and success.

Beginning with the end in mind, we will reflect on a new
vision for our schools, along with strategies to convert an obso-
lete system into a dynamic model of teaching and learning. We
will carefully consider the history of how our present system
was developed, not to criticize but to understand. Then we will
look at the learning and implementation challenges we may face
at every level of instruction and consider steps forward. Change
is challenging. Transformation is possible. And this is the time
for both in our schools.

Most educators who work in our schools are among the
most dedicated and compassionate people in the world. The
students who come to our schools need us to do better, not by
adding more pressure to our existing structure, but by
re-conceptualizing our system to meet the needs of modern
learners. Learning outcomes have never been more important.
This book suggests a change in the underlying architecture of
our design for education that will allow us to make teaching an
honor and pleasure and to help students fall in love with learning for life.

**We are at the inception of the most exciting time in the
history of education.** For those who are ready to innovate, the

opportunities to lead and create are endless. We have barely scratched the surface of the potential for human learning. Decades of discovery and transformation lie ahead, and some of you reading this book will likely lead the way. From the ashes of decades of failed school reform, you will construct education systems that bring learning alive for our children, offer the most effective antidote to poverty, bring respect and collegiality back to the profession of teaching, and create a more productive and peaceful world for all our children.

1

Looking Back, a Parent's Remembrance

When it was time for Matt to go to preschool, we picked a school with a great reputation, a calm and thoughtful school culture, with some really good teachers. But even though we believed we had chosen well, we were surprised when they showed us their system for tracking progress toward important early childhood competencies. These outcomes included all aspects of development, and we knew they'd be paying careful attention to oral language, sensory-motor, social, behavior and self-regulation, and self-care skills, along with early literacy and numeracy skills. The teachers promised to keep track of his skill development so they'd never overlook something crucial, and they would know how to challenge him enough but never too much. It amazed us how well they knew our boy and how we were included in the planning process and able to learn more about what to do with our son at home.

By the time he was old enough for kindergarten, he had exceeded the standard for competency in several of the domains of early childhood, he loved school, and he loved learning. It was hard to leave that preschool, but they helped us find an elementary program that picked right up where they had left off.

The elementary school took Matt's inventory of competent skills and knew right where to focus on his learning needs and strengths. By the middle of his kindergarten year, he was happily working on first grade math. It took him a little longer to reach the standard for proficiency in self-regulation, and his hand-eye skills needed some extra practice, but the teacher knew his ability levels and gave him exactly what he needed. It was like that all through the early grades. Sometimes, he joined kids from another grade for reading and math groups.

Amazingly, these teachers never seemed rushed. We worried about that, since many of the schools we'd visited seemed to be highly stressed environments in which teachers raced through their lessons and never let kids play. But in Matt's school, it wasn't like that. There was time for activities, projects, music, nature, and art. The teachers had well-established routines that included time for talking and developing social skills.

We wondered sometimes, and once we asked the teacher if they should be pushing Matt harder. She smiled like she'd heard that question many times before. Then she explained that by knowing her students well, she could give them just enough challenge without pushing them into the frustration zone. It made sense, and she showed us the school's test scores. Pushing kids beyond their abilities makes kids shut down. In addition to better test scores in the short run, she explained, the work they were doing was more likely to help Matt love math, love reading and writing, and love learning for the rest of his life. He thrived in those early childhood years.

By Matt's fourth grade year, he had a solid learning foundation, and the school had developed a profile of his skills. They showed us the learning steps that lead to competency or competency-plus in mathematics, technology, social science, reading, writing, cultural awareness, personal health, social-emotional development, career development, service learning, arts and science. Kids could take all the time and get all the support needed to become proficient at every step along the pathways to competency. Even kids from less fortunate backgrounds flourished in this school. All they needed was a chance.

From that point forward, Matt had a personalized learning plan that took into account his interests and needs, the recommendations of his teachers, and the things we thought were most important for our son. Science was broken up into modules, and he didn't just learn so he could pass a test; he learned so he could really understand. There were no grades. It was all about deep understanding, and he could take as much time as needed to develop a new technology skill, math skill, or learn a new form of writing.

At some point during the middle school years, Matt discovered the microbiome. Something about the balance of bacteria and other critters living in the gut fascinated him. So his teachers found lots of ways to incorporate learning about the microbiome into his math, science, geography, writing, and reading activities. It was exciting watching his learning profile as he progressed along the pathways to competency. There were so many options for learning. At school, there were modules of instruction, lots of mini-courses for enrichment or exploration, community and nature projects, sports and extracurricular activities, and even internships. There were online learning options for both home and school. Community members were brought in to be module instructors for special topics.

During all those years, I never once heard Matt or his friends talk about wanting to find an easy course or an easy teacher. The whole concept of wanting to get a good grade without having to give much effort was gone from the schools. Learning was for a purpose, and there was no such thing as pretend-competency. You were competent when you had the knowledge and skills and could apply them in complex ways. Or you weren't. Occasionally Matt would slack off a bit, but slackers did not gain new skills, and he'd come quickly around.

By the time he got to high school, Matt was already close to meeting the standards for graduation in a couple of the domains of learning, but his personalized plan allowed for him to advance as soon as he was ready. He was able to extend his learning through volunteer work in the community and by taking on a couple of apprenticeships. For the students in this high school, learning was a mix of modules taught at school, blended-learning modules, apprenticeship and internships, project-based learning, community college technical programs, and international cohort groups for special projects. Because of the personalized learning plans and the competency profiles, the line between high school and post-secondary education was pretty blurred. Some of his classes were at the community college, and others were in the basement of one of the technology companies in our town.

For us as parents, one of the greatest joys was watching him take charge of his own learning. Sure there were minimum competencies he had to reach, but Matt got to choose the skills for which he wanted to achieve something better than competency. There were so many paths to competency and beyond competency. He was able to find the areas of knowledge and skill that fascinated him, and so his interest in learning continued to grow. By the time he graduated high school, there were no more GPAs at his school. That was considered an old school concept from another age. In addition to a high school diploma, he'd earned competencies and certificates from the community college and from one of our state universities.

The high schools, community colleges, and state and private universities had worked out a system of verified competencies and shared learning pathways. Degrees and certificates no longer measured seat time and credits but instead reflected whether a student had the skills, knowledge, and application represented by a specific degree. You could finish a program in six months or three years and finishing meant something.

Matt has advanced certificates and degrees now, but he's not done learning. Some of his learning is facilitated by one of the universities, but often it's the product of a network of professionals our son has come to know from around the world. It's all about learning, he says. Sometimes he teaches a module at the middle or high school. He really likes that. In his own work, he does research and often collaborates with one of the local hospitals.

We have two grandchildren now and another on the way. These kids will never be forced to endure the old curriculum-driven, one-size-fits-all, seat time, and Carnegie credit system. They'll never be rewarded with a good grade for picking an easy teacher or a blow off class. Our grandkids will recognize that we all learn differently, in our own way and at our own pace. They will understand that learning is too precious to consider making kids race through content they don't understand, memorize facts and protocols to pass a test, or sit through months of boring lessons they already understand.

Our grandchildren will see learning as a beautiful challenge, a privilege, and a lifelong pursuit. From the preschool that carefully builds the foundation of learning, to the years in which they discover their own special interests, to the years in which they extend knowledge and collaborate with learners around the globe, these children will walk down the pathways to competency.

(Note: This story is a fable. Someday it will be the true story of the learning lives of many children.)

2

Informed Instruction Leads to Competency, Part One

Careful observation, followed by an informed choice, watchful monitoring of progress toward essential outcomes, and then more choices about how to encourage, teach, or intervene for our kids—that is informed instruction.

With a toddler learning to walk, we hold her hand. We check the surroundings for safety and let go at just the right time to watch her step forward on her own. With a child learning to throw and catch, we assess his skills, decide whether to use the beanbag or the larger playground ball, and then throw carefully so that the ball is easily catchable. We carefully consider our choice of a book for an early reader. Then, we sit close and practice reading, carefully observing whether the experience of reading this book is interesting, highly successful, and fun.

Informed instruction is our best attempt to give kids what they need at their level of readiness. A good coach knows the skills of her players and designs practice activities that are challenging but never so difficult that the kids get frustrated and quit trying. A teenager learning to drive gets up early on a Sunday morning. Dad drives with him to the high school parking lot. No one is there. The lot is empty. No cars to hit. No distractions. This is an opportunity to safely practice beginning driving skills.

Informed instruction includes the identification of all the steps needed to reach our goal. When teaching a child to build and fly a kite, we plan the steps carefully. We lay out the paper together and then cautiously attach it to the frame of the kite, making every inch secure. We attach the string and tail, giving the child as much independence as possible but checking each step and suggesting changes as needed. Once outside, we show our kids how to check the wind and consider in which direction we should lay out the kite. We check for power lines and other obstacles. And then it is time to learn to run into the face of the wind and watch the kite rise far above us.

Crucial instruction does not take shortcuts. Competency is competency. When teaching our kids to ride a bike, we carefully judge their readiness and then offer sufficient instruction and practice every step of the way.

When the outcomes are really important, we find ways to use informed instruction which leads to competency. When training a pilot to fly, we ensure that there is sufficient training, practice, and many demonstrations of competency before he is allowed to fly alone or with passengers. When you hire a master electrician, you know they have had a supervised training program, served as an apprentice, and demonstrated competency in every essential skill.

Medical doctors do not complete their training by taking a class in which they receive an overview of surgery or an introduction to the use of medications. Covering content is not enough to ensure competence. In any general or specialty area of practice, they are expected to demonstrate that they have both the knowledge and the skills. The crucial skills are clearly delineated.

As their skills develop, they are allowed to move forward to more complex applications of skill. If their skills are poor, they find tutors and mentors, and they improve, or they wash out of the program. To get their degrees, they must pass rigorous practical assessments and demonstrate competency.

Most of our Pre-K to Grade 12 schools, unfortunately, are not models of informed instruction leading to competency. For more than a century, we have used a curriculum-driven model of instruction that includes long lists of content to cover in each grade and, in recent years, has added the pressure of high-stakes standardized assessment. We use rigid pacing guides that require teachers to stay up with the expected rate of coverage. Some schools use scripted learning programs that demand that every child receives the same instruction at the same time. We expect teachers to cover more content than humanly possible, and we expect all kids to keep up.

If we used a rigidly paced system like ours while building a house, the results would not be pretty. With a timetable that doesn't allow for sick workers or bad weather, the foundation would not yet be complete when it is time to begin working on the frame. Because the foundation is unfinished and uneven, building the frame gets more complicated. When it is time to put on the drywall, the frame is sloppy, and the plumbing and electrical are unfinished. But a timetable is a timetable, and the workers are required to move forward and stay on schedule. The plumbing leaks, and the electrical system does not work; the drywall is uneven and unpainted. But it is time for the house to go on sale. How long would this construction company stay in business?

Some learning outcomes are crucial. These deserve careful assessment of student readiness, informed instruction at the student's instructional level, and all the time, instruction and intervention needed for the development of complete competency. Another way of expressing this: take your time with the important stuff.

For example, early learning success is crucial to long-term learning success, and key skills in the development of language, literacy, numeracy, motor skills, and behavior and self-regulation skills deserve the support needed to achieve competency. In math, there are key skills that build the foundation of number sense that is needed to understand and enjoy math for life. Behavior and self-regulation skills are as important as any academic skill in predicting long-term learning success but are not tested on any state or national standardized assessment. Nonetheless, they are crucial and deserve to be developed to competency.

Every crucial skill that builds the foundation for lifelong learning success deserves a competency based learning approach. Every key skill along the pathway to crucial learning outcomes deserves a competency based learning approach.

> This book examines the basic model of instruction we've used for more than a century and finds it lacking. Rather than asking teachers to teach more or teach faster, we seek ways to work smarter.

We seek better outcomes for our students, so that they have the skills and behaviors to be successful lifelong learners in the information age. This requires a love of learning based on successful learning experiences, as well as the competent skills needed to move forward to learning outcomes that allow us to live socially and financially flourishing lives.

The divide between the rich and the poor is growing in our country. This growing disparity is in part based on family affluence and opportunity, but much of it is based on the gap in learning competencies.

High-quality oral language skills, literacy skills, numeracy skills, and motor skills matter. Self-regulation, the ability to self-calm, focus, persist, delay gratification, and adjust your mood and behavior to meet the situation, matter. Competent skills for scientific thinking and self-directed learning matter. In the land of opportunity, competency is the primary antidote to poverty.

Competency based learning and informed instruction are not new concepts. We use these concepts at home every day as we raise our children. We use them in educational institutions that serve professions in which competence is perceived as crucial.

Today, learning success is crucial for all our children. No longer can we afford to rely on a system that is designed for only a small percentage to become highly skilled learners. Our children and our professional educators deserve a thoughtful learning model that helps develop calm classrooms, motivated and successful kids, teachers who are proud of their success, and informed instruction toward competency in every crucial outcome that can affect the learning lives of our children.

3

The Curriculum-Driven Model

The systems design for American public schools was significantly influenced by the work of Horace Mann and Frederick Winslow Taylor. Mann was the Secretary of the first Massachusetts State Board of Education. In 1843, he traveled to Europe to study the education systems of the time and, after his return, supported the adoption of the Prussian education system, which became the adopted system in Massachusetts, then New York, and eventually the other states. The Prussian system provided an eight-year course of primary education and emphasized the skills needed in an early-industrialized world (reading, writing, and arithmetic) along with education in ethics, duty, discipline, and obedience. Affluent children often went on to attend preparatory private schools for an additional four years, but most children did not advance beyond eighth grade (Downs, 1974; Taylor, 2010).

Mann was also the founder of the *Common School Journal*, in which he offered six main principles for public education:

- ♦ The public should no longer remain ignorant;
- ♦ Public education should be paid for, controlled, and sustained by an interested public;
- ♦ Public education will be best provided in schools that embrace children from a variety of backgrounds;

- ◆ Public education must be non-sectarian;
- ◆ Education must be taught by the spirit, methods, and discipline of a free society;
- ◆ Education should be provided by well-trained, professional teachers.

Frederick Winslow Taylor was an American inventor and engineer who developed a set of management principles, in which waste is avoided and production is improved, called scientific management theory. His efficiency principles are described in his book *The Principles of Scientific Management* (1911).

He studied the motions required to complete a task, devised a way to break the task down into component motions, and looked for the most efficient and effective manner to do the work. This was described as "the one best way." Taylor recommended enforced standardization of methods, a clear distinction between management and workers, and strong management control (Kanigel, 1997).

The influence of Taylor is seen in the organization and management of schools in the early parts of the 20th century. The development of curriculum, grade level learning material, and standard delivery of instruction reflect the philosophy of Taylor. Students were organized into classrooms by grades, in spite of what we see today as significant variance among the learning readiness of same-age students. Instruction was organized into subject areas, separating social studies from reading, math from science. Standard units of time (class periods) were used to separate subject areas and give the same time to each subject. Teachers were separated into classrooms designed for teacher-directed coverage of grade level curricula. The distinction between teaching staff and administration was clearly delineated and reinforced by pay, power, and prestige.

Taylor's influence on the design of our schools has persisted over time. We still separate kids by grade, cover standardized curricula by subject matter, create pacing guides to keep teachers on track, offer credits by measuring seat time, and confer graduation diplomas that measure the number of credits rather than the learning skills of our students. Students are subjected to "the one best way" of standardized instruction, which is incredibly boring for some and frustrating and impossible for others.

Google, Intel, Starbucks, Quicken, Apple, and most modern businesses have long ago rejected the strict standardization of Taylor's methodology. Collaboration, continuous learning, and innovation are the canons of modern business. Modern businesses must learn and adapt to survive. They recognize the acceleration of learning when teams of people collaborate. They recognize the importance of business culture and a sense of community on the effectiveness of their employees.

> Today's mantra in a thriving business is learn, adapt, experiment, and improve within a culture that encourages respect and collaboration. Public schools have continued to use "the one best way" of standardized delivery of grade level content objectives, with little professional collaboration or innovation.

Mann promoted public education for all using the Prussian teacher-directed and grade-based model. Taylor sought to add efficiency by standardizing instruction by age/grade, subject matter, separation of classrooms, and by establishing a clear distinction between the influence and authority of teachers and administration. In this system, learning is measured by seat time and credits earned, and instruction is delivered in the same way to all students.

In schools we continue to use a one-hundred-year-old systems model that successful modern businesses have largely abandoned.

4

Standardized Delivery of Instruction

In 1900, the rate of graduation from high school in the United States was 6.4 percent. By 1910, it had risen slightly to 8.8 percent (EPE Research Center, 2010; US Census Bureau, 2014a). For most folks, primary level education was enough. The advantages of advanced levels of learning were not enough to motivate large numbers of students and their families to make the choice to stay in school. A strong back and a good work ethic were enough for the demands of most jobs.

In the context of the early 1900s, public education existed comfortably with the cover and sort methods that are part of the curriculum-driven model. With a vast majority of students not going beyond eighth grade, and with jobs not dependent on advanced learning skills, there was no pressure for all students to succeed in school. High rates of literacy and mathematical skill were not required in the workplace.

Taylor's principles of efficiency worked well enough within the needs of the early 1900s. The development of a standard curriculum, grade level learning material, and pacing expectations for each course went unquestioned, even as large numbers of students were uninspired and unsuccessful in the classroom. With the influence of Thorndike and others, the use of testing became a greater part of the educational model.

In the economic and social context of the early 1900s, as public education and compulsory schooling were still developing, the use of a standardized curriculum and testing system made sense. Students were exposed to content without any serious commitment to helping all students become highly successful or lifelong learners.

Public education focused on the efficient design and delivery of instruction using a one-size-fits-all model. Many students were left behind because of developmental differences, experience differences, and language differences, but it did not matter to society as long as many jobs did not require higher levels of learning skill.

> Sorting students into bluebirds and blackbirds may have been hurtful to individual students, but society had plenty of room for blackbirds.

After World War II, industrial innovation and the development of new technologies began to change the face of business. Interest in improved learning outcomes increased, and high school graduation and college entry rates began to rise significantly. Many more people saw education as important for their own lives and for the lives of their children.

But as the perceived importance of education increased, we held onto our familiar model of instruction: efficient delivery of a standard curriculum. Using the same old design for instruction, we responded to the pressure for better outcomes by speeding up the assembly line. We added more content, much more. Teachers are now expected to cover more content in the time allotted. We shifted some of this content to younger age-range delivery, which means that content once delivered in fourth grade may now be covered in second grade. We added testing systems to hold teachers and schools accountable.

> As the importance of literacy, math, science, technology, problem-solving, and the ability to continue learning throughout life increased, we held onto our familiar model of standardized delivery of instruction.
>
> We cover, we test, we move on. Students are sorted by whether they can keep up with the curriculum.

As job requirements became more complex, business leaders called for improvements in public education. Public attention to the results of international testing data added even more pressure on our schools, as American children fell conspicuously behind other nations. Politicians joined into the fray, imposing additional reporting and testing requirements. National data showed discrepancies among racial subgroups and between the affluent and the poor, and more pressure came to bear. We've federalized the assessment systems, adopted national standards for curriculum, and imposed evaluation structures in which teachers are judged by student test scores.

The pressure to improve learning outcomes in our schools has been building for decades, and still we operate within the basic systems design of Horace Mann and Frederick Winslow Taylor, a system that prioritizes efficient delivery and testing of a standard curriculum. We cover, we test, and we move on. Students are sorted by whether they keep up with the curriculum. We deliver more content, and we deliver it faster, and we test it more rigorously, but it is the same basic system design we've used for more than a hundred years.

5

Failing to Meet Society's Learning Needs

For many years, when high levels of skill in math, science, and reading were crucial for only a privileged few, the curriculum-driven system successfully sorted out the less fortunate, motivated, or talented learners with no ill effects on society. A small group of educated men and women was enough. The education model based on coverage, grading, and sorting worked well enough to meet our needs.

The learning needs of our society are no longer well served by this model. The requirements of medium- and high-wage jobs include math, reading, technical skills, problem-solving skills, collaboration skills, and the capacity to continue to learn and keep up with new information and technical advances. Being a successful learner, and developing the capacity for intrinsically motivated learning, has never been more crucial for the financial and social future of individual students. Becoming a nation in which most students are successful learners has never been more important to the economic future of our society.

The cover, test, and sort (CTS) instructional delivery system of a hundred years ago, even in its present juiced-up form, is not producing outcomes which are good for society, good for individuals, or fair to students with fewer advantages at home.

Using our curriculum-driven approach, about 79 percent of all public high school students graduate on time; about 70 percent of economically disadvantaged students graduate on time (NCES, 2014). In the information age, these 20 to 30 percent of young men and women who drop out of high school face low-skill, low-wage options and challenging futures.

According to the NAEP (2013) among 12th grade students (remember that a significant group of students has already dropped out by this point), 26 percent score at or above proficient levels in math, and 38 percent are proficient or better in reading. Among African American 12th grade students tested, 7 percent are proficient or better in math, and 16 percent are proficient or better in reading. Students who manage to graduate but do not have proficient skills face great challenges in college or technical training and even greater challenges in the workplace.

Those students who go to college are typically thought of as learning success stories. College has often been considered the passageway to good jobs and financial opportunity. Rates of college attendance have climbed steadily over the last several decades. In 2012, among 18- to 24-year-olds, 41 percent were enrolled in a two- or four-year degree-granting institution (NCES, 2014).

But many college and university students are finding a more difficult path. Some students are not academically equipped for advanced education. Others lack the focus, attention, and persistence needed to go to class, study consistently, and make the choices needed to succeed in school.

The 2011 graduation rate for full-time, first-time undergraduate students who began their pursuit of a bachelor's degree at a 4-year degree-granting institution in fall 2005 was 59 percent. That is, 59 percent of full-time, first-time students who began seeking a bachelor's degree at a 4-year institution in fall 2005 completed the degree at that institution within six years (NCES, 2014).

In recent years, even college grads have had difficulty finding employment in their field of training. Forbes Magazine reports that 60 percent of college graduates cannot find full-time work in their chosen profession (Forbes, 2012). Employers point to a skills gap and a lack of the necessary business and technical skills, along with poor interpersonal skills, appearance, punctuality, and flexibility.

Bloomberg (2012) reports that since 2011 companies have reported more than 3 million job openings each month, according to the Department of Labor. But with 13 million Americans looking for work and 8 million more settling for part-time jobs, many of these millions of jobs continue to go unfilled due to the lack of match between skill requirements and the available workforce.

The CTS delivery model is designed to cover, test, and sort. It was never designed to nurture competency in a majority of students or to help large numbers of kids fall in love with learning for life. Lacking a model in which essential learning outcomes are identified and then carefully developed, we have continued to pursue coverage and testing with vigor.

- By the beginning of fourth grade, only 34 percent of American children are at proficient reading levels (NAEP, 2013);
- Only 20 percent of fourth grade children who are eligible for free or reduced lunch are at proficient reading levels (NAEP, 2013);
- About 79 percent of all public high school students graduate on time; about 70 percent of economically disadvantaged students graduate on time (NCES, 2014);
- Among 12th grade students (remember that a significant group of students has already dropped out by this point), 26 percent score at or above proficient levels in math, and 38 percent are proficient or better in reading (NAEP, 2013);
- Among African American 12th grade students tested, 7 percent are proficient or better in math, and 16 percent are proficient or better in reading (NAEP, 2013);
- The Joint Chiefs of Staff report that about 75 percent of the country's 17- to 24-year-olds are ineligible for military service (Mission Readiness, 2009);

- Of full-time, first-time students who began seeking a bachelor's degree at a four-year institution in fall 2005, 59 percent completed the degree at that institution within six years (NCES, 2014);
- 60 percent of college graduates cannot find full-time work in their chosen profession (Forbes, 2012);
- With 13 million Americans looking for work and 8 million more settling for part-time jobs, 3 million jobs continue to go unfilled due to the lack of match between skill requirements and the available workforce (Forbes, 2012).

Using our present CTS model, we continue to produce astonishing numbers of struggling K-12 students, high school dropouts, dropouts from institutions of advanced learning, and college grads without the skills to compete in the workplace. How could it be any different?

6

Making the Case for Change

The American Dream—the idea that anyone who is determined and works hard can get ahead—has long defined the promise of the United States. Yet the reality is that life chances for Americans are now determined to a significant degree by the wealth of our parents. The dream that hard work and playing by the rules will lead to greater opportunity and a steady climb up the economic ladder is increasingly challenging to achieve, particularly for struggling families.

—Annie E. Casey Foundation (2014)

Hard work still counts, but hard work without competency in academic, social-emotional, and technical skills is unlikely to be enough to find success in the information and technology economy. Auto factories, which once employed thousands of men and women, now operate with a staff of hundreds, each with technical skills and responsibilities. Farmers, tool and die makers, service providers, and manufacturers increasingly rely on equipment that requires reading and computing and on employees who can regularly learn to use new systems and procedures.

While millions of low-skill workers compete for low-wage jobs, more than 3 million jobs that require high-skill workers go unfilled in the American economy.

With our continued reliance on the CTS model, only a small segment of our society becomes proficient in reading and math, develops a deep love of learning, becomes intrinsically motivated to learn throughout life, has strong social-emotional skills, and has the self-regulation and character skills to focus and persevere. For these few, living in the information age is rich with opportunity.

In 2011, 48 percent of income went to the top 10 percent of earners, and 19 percent of income went to the top 1 percent; in comparison, the top 1 percent took home 8 percent of total income in the 1970s. The top 1 percent own 40 percent of the nation's financial wealth, while the bottom 80 percent own only 7 percent (OECD, 2011). Over the last 30 years, the bottom 60 percent of the population has seen their wealth decline, while the top 5 percent has grown increasingly richer (US Census Bureau, 2014b). This can be understood in large part based on the staggering differences in learning success rates among students, which correlate to rates of affluence.

By relying as we do on the Cover Test Sort methodology of our curriculum-driven schools, the effects of poverty on school success and life success will continue to haunt generations of students. Unless schools and parents step up to the responsibility to help far more of our children develop competency in the skills that could allow them to become successful learners and to earn a decent job, poverty will increasingly beget learning failure and more poverty. Without skills that matter to employers, most poor children are doomed to economic and social hardship. Without rock-solid learning skills, poor children face lives of struggle.

> Determination and hard work, without the skills of learning, no longer lead to success. That day is gone. A new day has arrived, in which learning success must be part of the formula for success, part of the path toward the American dream.

We live in a time of incredible opportunity. Information has gone from scarce to superabundant. New ideas, new discoveries, and new products are commonplace. Sophisticated quantitative analysis is being applied to building airplanes and to shopping at Target. A world of opportunity awaits students with good learning skills, a love of learning, an intrinsically motivated desire to learn, collaboration skills, social-emotional skills, communication skills, technical skills, self-regulation skills, and the qualities of character to make it all work.

The importance of a new set of skills and competencies for a more effective workforce has been recognized for decades. In 1991, US Secretary of Labor Lynn Martin convened the Secretary's Commission on Achieving Necessary Skills (SCANS), asking an esteemed committee to define the skills needed for employment, propose acceptable levels of proficiency, suggest effective ways to assess proficiency, and develop a dissemination strategy for the nation's schools, businesses, and homes.

Their report described both foundation skills and competencies needed for workplace success. Even though this commission completed its work decades ago, its recommendations are a clear voice for a focus on developing competencies needed for success at work and in life (National Technical Information Service, 1991).

The SCANS Advised Parents

Parents must insist that their sons and daughters master this know-how and that their local schools teach it. Unless you do, your children are unlikely to earn a decent living. If your children cannot learn these skills by the time they leave high school, they face bleak prospects—dead-end work, interrupted only by periods of unemployment, with little chance to climb a career ladder.

SCANS Recommendations

The know-how identified by SCANS is made up of five competencies and a three-part foundation of skills and personal qualities that are needed for solid job performance. These include (Table excerpted from *What Work Requires of Schools: A SCANS Report for America 2000*, US Department of Labor, June 1991, pp. iii.):

⚑ COMPETENCIES—effective workers can productively use:

◆ Resources—allocating time, money, materials, space, and staff;
◆ Interpersonal Skills—working on teams, teaching others, serving customers, leading, negotiating, and working well with people from culturally diverse backgrounds;
◆ Information—acquiring and evaluating data, organizing and maintaining files, interpreting and communicating, and using computers to process information;
◆ Systems—understanding social, organizational, and technological systems, monitoring and correcting performance, and designing or improving systems;
◆ Technology—selecting equipment and tools, applying technology to specific tasks, and maintaining and troubleshooting technologies.

⚑ THE FOUNDATION—competence requires:

◆ Basic Skills—reading, writing, arithmetic and mathematics, speaking, and listening;
◆ Thinking Skills—thinking creatively, making decisions, solving problems, seeing things in the mind's eye, knowing how to learn, and reasoning;
◆ Personal Qualities—individual responsibility, self-esteem, sociability, self-management, and integrity.

Since SCANS, many individuals and organizations have contributed ideas to the discussion of what specific skills should be regarded as crucial 21st century skills. The Partnership for 21st Century Skills, the Educational Policy Improvement Center, the Change Leadership Group at the Harvard Graduate School of Education, ASCD, and the Global Education and Skills Forum, to name a few, have offered their insights to this discussion. You may wish to add some of your own ideas to the mix.

Critical thinking, problem solving, reasoning, analysis, interpretation, synthesizing information, research skills, interrogative questioning, creativity, artistry, curiosity, imagination, innovation, personal expression, self-calming, attentional skills, perseverance, self-direction, planning, self-discipline, adaptability, initiative, oral and written communication, public speaking and presenting, listening, leadership, teamwork, collaboration, cooperation, virtual workspaces, balance, agility, bilateral motor skills, visual motor integration, information and communication technology (ITC) literacy, media and internet literacy, visual interpretation, data interpretation and analysis, computer programming, civic, ethical and social-justice literacy, cultural awareness, economic and financial literacy, entrepreneurialism, global awareness, multicultural literacy, humanitarianism, scientific literacy and reasoning, the scientific method, environmental and conservation literacy, ecosystems understanding, health and wellness literacy, including nutrition, diet, exercise, public health and safety.

The danger, of course, is that we will develop one more amazing list of things to do/cover in school, that we will add more mandates and more tests, maybe a few more pacing guides. The danger is that we will treat crucial 21st century skills using our coverage-based delivery model, without helping each child clearly identify the skills that must be carefully developed, one step at a time, until competent skills have been fully developed.

7

Giving Up Unproductive Mental Models

So much of what we do in schools is based on continuing familiar patterns of belief and behavior. Here are a few ideas whose time is up.

Equating Quantity with Quality

In 1983, the President's Commission on Excellence in Education published its report, *A Nation at Risk: The Imperative for Educational Reform*. The report famously stated, "The educational foundations of our society are presently being eroded by a rising tide of mediocrity that threatens our very future as a Nation and a people. If an unfriendly foreign power had attempted to impose on America the mediocre educational performance that exists today, we might well have viewed it as an act of war." The report supported the idea that American schools were failing and touched off a wave of state and federal reform efforts that continue to this day. The 1989 Bush Education Summit, Goals 2000, NCLB, Race to the Top, and ESEA waivers are rooted in the same political soil, based on the belief that legislative action and Department of Education regulations could improve education outcomes.

Under pressure, the curriculum-driven assembly line model responded by doing more of what a curriculum-driven assembly line model does. We added more content expectations. We asked teachers to cover content more quickly. We added more testing to ensure that all the content was being covered. We added pacing guides and district pacing assessments. Many schools adopted scripted, one-size-fits-all reading and math programs to ensure that everything was being covered. We began to grade and fail schools. We began to require evaluation of teachers based on student learning outcomes.

Teachers have felt the pressure to "cover" for several decades. In a comparison of US curricula to that of high achieving countries (Schmidt et al., 2001; Schmidt, Wang, & McKnight, 2005; Schmidt & Cogan, 2009), the number of science and math topics covered in US schools is significantly greater, and the amount of repetition of content from grade to grade is almost double that of the better achieving school systems.

Schmoker and Marzano (1999) advise educators, "We will realize the promise of school reform when we establish standards and expectations for reaching them that are clear, not confusing; essential, not exhaustive. The result will be a new coherence and a shared focus that could be the most propitious step we can take toward educating all students well."

Viable content is the content that can be reasonably covered in the time available. In *What Works in Schools* (2003), Robert Marzano ranks a guaranteed and viable content as the factor having the most impact on student achievement.

> If you wanted to teach all of the standards in the national documents, you would have to change schooling from K-12 to K-22.
> 255 standards across 14 subject areas
> 3,500 benchmarks
> 13,000 hours of class time available
> 9,000 hours of instruction available
> 15,500 hours of instruction needed to cover the 3,500 benchmarks
> —Robert Marzano (2003)

> The National Council of Teachers of Mathematics recommends that math curriculum should include fewer topics, spending enough time to make sure each is learned in enough depth that it need not be revisited in later grades. That is the approach used in most top-performing nations.
> —National Mathematics Advisory Council (2008)

In spite of consistent recommendations to slow down the pace of instruction, there is little evidence that anyone is listening. In recent years, the narrative to the Common Core State Standards calls over and over to us to cover fewer topics to a deeper level of understanding so that topics do not need to be retaught in subsequent grades. But the fear of not being ready for the mandated state and national tests seems to have limited our ability to respond thoughtfully and truly narrow the scope of instructional content.

According to *The Reality of College Readiness* (ACT, 2013), only 25 percent of the 1.8 million students taking the ACT exam are college-ready in math, reading, English, and science. More than one-fourth of ACT-tested graduates did not meet any of the four college readiness benchmarks. ACT has defined "college and career readiness" as the acquisition of knowledge and skills a student needs to enroll and succeed in credit-bearing first-year college courses at a postsecondary institution without the need for remediation.

Ready, Willing and Unable to Serve (2009), a report prepared for the Joint Chiefs of Staff, concludes that about 75 percent of the country's 17- to 24-year-olds are ineligible for military service, largely because they are poorly educated, overweight, or have physical ailments that make them unfit for the armed forces. The Joint Chiefs have called this a national security issue. Those days when the armed services welcome young men and women with behavior and learning problems are gone.

The Programme for International Student Assessment (OECD, 2012) compares learning outcomes among the world's more economically developed countries. Among the 34 OECD countries, 15-year-old students from the US ranked 27th in math, just below Spain, the Russian Federation, and the Slovak Republic. US students ranked 17th in reading and 20th in science.

> In a recent report by the Educational Testing Service, *America's Skills Challenge: Millennials and the Future* (2015), the ETS compared literacy, numeracy, and problem solving skills of 16- to 34-year-olds in 22 countries using data from the OECD Programme for International Assessment of Adult Competencies. In literacy, US millennials scored lower than 15 other nations. In both numeracy and problem solving, US millennials were tied for last.

ETS's Irwin Kirsch, in the preface to the report, stated:

This report suggests that far too many are graduating high school and completing postsecondary educational programs without receiving adequate skills. If we expect to have a better educated population and a more competitive workforce, policy makers and other stakeholders will need to shift the conversation from one of educational attainment to one that acknowledges the growing importance of skills and examines these more critically.
—ETS (2015)

By the beginning of fourth grade, the point at which we can accurately predict long-term learning outcomes, only 34 percent of American children are at proficient reading levels (National Assessment of Educational Progress, 2013; National Center for Education Statistics, 2015a). Only 20 percent of children who are eligible for free or reduced lunch are at proficient reading levels. The vast majority of these fourth grade non-proficient learners are *unlikely* to become good readers, love to learn, succeed in advanced education, or become learners for life.

When it comes to human learning, quantity does not equate to quality. Our curriculum-driven instructional model, on steroids since the advent of national school reform initiatives, has consistently failed to help more students love learning or to attain high levels of skill in literacy, numeracy, or problem solving. The poor are especially vulnerable to the adverse effects of this model, but all students suffer from our continued reliance on this design for teaching and learning.

Grading on the Bell Curve

In probability theory, normal (or Gaussian) distribution is typically described by use of a bell curve, which shows the mean and standard variation from the mean. One deviation from the mean is comprised of approximately one-third of the total, and everything within one standard deviation up and one standard deviation down is statistically normal.

The bell curve is an important statistical tool used to analyze large sets of data, to determine what is typical, and to predict probable outcomes. In education, the use of the bell curve was adopted to determine normal distribution and assign grades based on a comparison with other students (Figure 7.1).

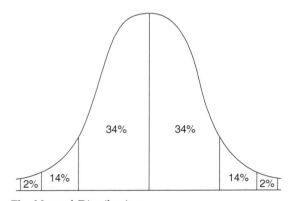

FIGURE 7.1 The Normal Distribution

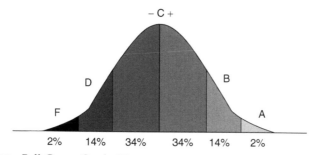

FIGURE 7.2 Bell Curve Grade Chart

When used for grading, a bell curve (Figure 7.2) ensures a balanced distribution of grades, with only a small percentage receiving the highest or the lowest grades. Over the years, mostly in response to pressure from parents, the grading "curve" has shifted to include far more B's and A's than the standard distribution.

The Gaussian Distribution is the statistical foundation for all of our state and national standardized testing. Numeric scores on standardized assessments are coverted to percentiles. At the 50th percentile, half the scores are better and half the scores are worse. At the 90th percentile, your score is better than 90 percent of the other scores. At the 10th percentile, your score is better than 10 percent of the other scores.

Use of a bell curve for grading can be misleading. As an example, imagine two high school English Language Arts instructors. One is an experienced and highly professional teacher who diligently pursues high-level reading and writing skills for her students. The other teacher has been waiting for retirement for the past decade, does no class preparation, and often reads the newspaper in class. Both classes are receiving instruction in English, but the quality of instruction and learning varies significantly. In both classes there is a normal distribution of grades, based on a loosely applied bell curve model. In the more professional teacher's classroom, eight students earned an A grade. In the less professional teacher's classroom, eight students earned an A grade. But a careful analysis of reading and writing skills shows that B students in the professional teacher's class have far better writing skills than A students in the slacker teacher's classroom.

> Coverage does not infer competency, and typical grading structures do not measure competency.

The bell curve is a tool for analyzing normal distribution among large sets of data, but it is not designed to tell which students are competent in any specific skill. In James' third grade math class, his teacher managed to "cover" every CCSS math standard. Using a math program in which all children get the same instruction on the same day in exactly the same way, the instructional plan directed the teacher to "cover" every content standard. There was no identification of essential math skills or concepts, and therefore no systematic measurement of progress toward these crucial outcomes. From week to week the teacher delivered lessons without going back to help needy students understand important skills at a deeper level.

Grades were awarded based on a bell curve model, identifying some as A math students and some as D math students. A few of the students had a very poor understanding of important math concepts but were great at memorizing facts and formulas. They scored well on tests. They received A's or B's. But their lack of deep understanding of important skills and concepts will likely cause them difficulty when they reach higher levels of math, for which memory of facts will not suffice.

At the end of the third grade, each child was given a D, C, B, or A in math. James was identified as a B- student in math. Not bad, he thought, compared with some of the other kids, not realizing that he had not yet fully developed key math skills even close to competency. Not realizing that math learning in the future would soon become difficult and frustrating. Not realizing that compromised development of crucial math skills would limit his working options for the rest of his life.

Creating Winners and Losers

There are times when rigorous coverage is a useful tool for sorting out which students should be allowed to continue in a program and which should not. Astronaut training puts candidates through a difficult course of training to decide which candidates have the right stuff. The first phases of training for medical doctors are purposefully difficult and serve to sort some students out of the process.

Navy Seals and Army Rangers go through an incredibly demanding series of training activities, and the vast majority of candidates do not make it. But the ones who do make it are the best candidates for these dangerous and demanding jobs.

When the program or profession only needs a small number of new members, and many people would like to be among this group, rigorous coverage and training are one way to help sort out the candidates who are diligent, ready to learn, and resilient.

As kids, we played King of the Raft. The idea was to throw others off the raft and try not to be thrown off. Some crafty kids would wait in the water until the stronger kids were bruised and tired and then climb up when no one was watching to throw off their tired friends and claim victory. Last man standing. Dodge ball is based on the same principle. Who is quickest, strongest, and has the best aim?

> Curriculum-driven instruction fits nicely with the King of the Raft philosophy of schools. Teach fast and hard and see which kids survive.

Good students and bad students. Red birds and black birds. Honor society and all the rest. Good readers and kids who hate to read. Math geeks and the vast majority who avoid math in their lives and careers. We continue to use systems that identify students who are "good" at instruction that was presented at one moment in time. We create winners and losers rather than recognizing that children have differing learning experiences and learning rates and that from any starting point students can build high-quality learning skills that matter.

In 1910, when fewer than 10 percent of students graduated from high school, the curriculum-driven, one-size-fits-all model worked just fine. In the modern world, schools based on this model are harming many children. Educators communicate the expectations of our curriculum-driven model in a variety of ways.

- ◆ *I have to keep up with the pacing guide.*
- ◆ *I am expected to cover all the chapters.*
- ◆ *I can't wait around for just a few kids who don't get it.*
- ◆ *Spiraling.*
- ◆ *We have to get ready for the test.*
- ◆ *The government requires that we cover all this material.*
- ◆ *You are expected to already know how to do this.*
- ◆ *If you'd only concentrate.*
- ◆ *If you'd do your homework.*
- ◆ *If you'd come to school on time.*
- ◆ *If you didn't miss so many days.*
- ◆ *Today I am covering CCSS.MATH.CONTENT.6.RP.A.3.*

There are many ways to say it. *I am teaching the content, and you are expected to keep up. If you don't keep up, and more than two-thirds of you won't, it's on you. If you get sick and miss some days, or are the youngest in your class, or live in a chaotic home, or learn differently, or carry the burden of high levels of stress, you will probably get left behind.*

For decades, American schools have been engaged in a failed experiment, attempting to cram more content into a typical teaching day than humanly possible, asking children to learn overwhelming content at younger and younger ages, and not taking the time to help every child build the foundation skills needed for lifelong learning success. We race through instruction in the same way for all kids, give grades that judge you rather than help you identify the specific skills and concepts you need to learn, and create educational winners and losers, mostly losers.

Fifty years ago the United States had the best-educated workforce in the world. Since then we've created anxiety-filled classrooms in which children are less likely to fall deeply in love with learning and where thoughtful teachers struggle to love their work. We continued to use a "more is better, test it harder" system that compares outcomes but does not support the development of competency. We've created a system that aggressively identifies the winners from the losers but has not made any progress toward reducing the number of losers.

Building crucial learning skills is not a race. By carefully identifying and then slowing down the pace of instruction for essential skills, and by allowing every child to fully develop these skills, we could improve the learning future of our children. As we evolve from a curriculum-driven educational design to a competency based learning model, we will establish a different framework that clearly identifies crucial learning outcomes, considers the learning steps along a pathway to important life skills, tracks student progress toward crucial outcomes, personalizes instruction, and supports teachers as they offer instruction that meets the needs of each student.

8

When Coverage Is Enough

In my spare time I am reading a book about Thomas Jefferson. It's a wonderful book, describing his incredible life and accomplishments along with some of his challenges and foibles. This book is designed to "cover" many aspects of an intriguing man's life. I read it for pleasure. It makes me wonder.

Occasionally I like to view TED Talks. They offer introductions to new, challenging, or interesting ideas that relate to modern life, education, and technology. They share different perspectives, ideas, and bits of information that occasionally defy some of my assumptions.

For me, a well-taught course on the history of Russian literature would be interesting and might help me identify writers whose books I want to read. But in-depth knowledge of Russian literature is not crucial to the priority outcomes in my life. An overview would suffice for my purposes. If you plan to become a professor of Russian literature, you will need a lot more than an overview. In-depth knowledge of the history of Russia, political influences on the arts, and the lives of primary authors would be crucial for your success as a professor. So too might be your competency in oral language skills, social interaction skills, teaching skills, and academic writing skills.

If I took a pottery class for fun, and to discover whether it inspired me to make beautiful pots, competency outcomes would not be necessary. But if I decide to drop out of teaching and writing, and devote myself to the craft of pottery-making, competency would take on much greater importance.

There are so many learning opportunities for which an overview, an introduction, or some form of coverage is a wonderful instructional design. Not all learning must lead to specifically defined competencies. Much of learning should be based on curiosity, the intrinsic hunger to learn, the desire to understand.

It is a privilege and a joy to engage in independent learning, to explore our interests, to read great books, to take courses that expose us to bodies of knowledge. Many of us work hard, in part to have the time and opportunity to seek knowledge for the sake of knowledge and for the joy of learning. When learning outcomes are for pleasure, enrichment, or exploration, coverage may be enough.

> The challenge is to recognize that introductions, overviews, and coverage have a place in the design of teaching and learning systems, but that competent skills must also be predictable outcomes for large numbers of student citizens.

Competent learning skills mean something very different today than in the early 1900s. Reading skills matter for us all. Numeracy and problem solving matter. Critical thinking and learning skills for life are more relevant today and predict future economic, social, and personal outcomes in the lives of our children.

The curriculum-driven educational model was never designed to produce large numbers of competent learners for life. During the era of education reform, we've added to the volume of content expectations (coverage) and added pressure to the system by relying on high-stakes testing. Perversely, all this pressure has not helped us achieve better performance outcomes and, at the same time, has stripped much of the joy out of the learning process in our schools.

The desire to learn, to wonder, to imagine, to explore, and to be curious is such an important part of being human. Our high-pressure modern version of curriculum-driven schooling produces lousy testing outcomes and also sucks the joy out of teaching and learning.

As we develop competency based learning models, we can hope that we are able to remember important lessons from the past. Respect the natural love of learning that all young children exhibit. Build pathways to competency so that large numbers of children can develop the learning skills needed in the information society but also allow time for exploration that feeds our curiosity. The love of learning is an important ingredient for building learners for life.

9

Personalized Learning and Competency

A competency based learning system begins with the premise that we truly want each student to succeed. Rather than letting the pacing guide dictate the delivery of instruction, students move ahead toward crucial learning outcomes upon demonstrating the key learning milestones along the path to competency. Students will have as many learning opportunities as they need to develop these crucial skills, and each student is guaranteed to have the support needed to continue learning at their own pace as they progress toward crucial outcomes.

This learner-centered model is a significant departure from the more is better, test it harder, winners and losers system we have created in most of our schools. Delivering one-size-fits-all instruction and then sorting out a small percentage of successful learners no longer meets the needs of our society. With a better understanding of how kids learn, and with the information and technology systems that are now available, we can choose to track progress toward crucial outcomes and develop thoughtful pathways to mastery of the skills needed for learning and workplace success.

Much of this is just the application of common sense. In the non-school parts of our lives, whenever a learning goal has been identified as "crucial" we try hard to develop personalized competency based learning experiences for our children. When teaching a young child to throw and catch, we refuse to follow a pacing guide. Instead we take the time to play, ensure high rates of success, and gradually increase challenge without causing frustration and disengagement. When teaching a teenager to drive a car, wise parents take all the necessary time to practice driving in the school parking lot before moving to the side roads, and all the time needed on the side roads before moving to the main roads, and all the time needed on main roads before moving to the expressways, and all the time needed driving during good weather conditions until allowing your child to drive in more difficult weather.

> No rational adult would throw a small hard ball at a child who is not fully able to catch it. Why then does math instruction in most schools consistently throw hardballs at kids who aren't ready?

Math instruction is among the conspicuous failures of US schools. It is a classic example of too much content, delivered too fast, using a rigid pacing process, and advancing students to higher levels of learning without the deep understanding of fundamental concepts and skills needed for long-term success. Consider these kindergarten math skills, which are crucial for understanding higher-level math concepts:

◆ Has one-to-one correspondence for numbers 1–30;
◆ Understands combinations to 10;
◆ Recognizes number groups (2–10) without counting.

> One-to-one correspondence is the ability to count concrete objects or movements with accuracy. Some children can say the numerals in sequence but do not yet have the connection to associate "three" with three buttons, "four" with

four buttons, etc. Children lacking one-to-one correspondence might say a number without really understanding its value.

Understanding combinations to 10 includes the ability to use one-to-one correspondence to show you "four buttons", then add "two buttons" and quickly figure out that now there are "six buttons". Using real objects or movements, they can demonstrate any combination of numbers adding up to 10 or less.

Recognizing number groups (2–10) without counting is the ability to look at a domino, or a die, or any pattern of dots, beads, chairs, etc., and quickly name the value. This skill is sometimes called "subitizing" and assumes some understanding of both one-to-one correspondence and combinations.

In a personalized-learning kindergarten environment, children would be carefully monitored for the development of these crucial math skills. Instruction would be matched to the child's readiness, so that some children might practice counting objects, while other children are working combinations. Some children would likely develop every one of these skills by January, while others would need hands-on and movement-based activities for these skills until April or May. Only when a child can perform a skill easily, with a high rate of success, using a variety of learning materials, would they be considered competent.

Each child would be given as much time as needed and as much differentiated learning practice as needed for these essential learning outcomes until competency is well established. But classroom instruction might also include lessons that "introduce, cover, or explore" additional content including measurement, estimation, equations, sets, and many other topics that can be enjoyed in small groups, centers, or whole group settings. Instruction becomes a blend of exploration activities that build a general understanding of math, along with carefully designed and differentiated instruction aimed toward competency in the specifically designated essential learning outcomes.

In a curriculum-driven kindergarten learning environment, all children would be given the same lesson on the same day in the same way. Early in the year, maybe even from the first day, math instruction would be delivered using worksheets, without access to the touching, moving, feeling experiences which are integral to understanding these basic skills. Students would be encouraged to memorize facts they do not understand or follow a series of steps to get an answer they can only hope might be right. Many of these students would move on to higher grades lacking number sense, not really understanding combination or number values.

If math learning outcomes are important to a child's future **(and they are)**, some skills deserve the time, instruction, and attention to help every child develop competency. Throwing math hardballs at young children creates frustrated, math-phobic students who will disengage from math learning for life. American millennials, tied for last place among the 22 countries evaluated in the OECD Programme for International Assessment of Adult Competencies (ETS, 2015) in math and problem solving, give evidence of the poor outcomes associated with curriculum-driven math instruction.

Competency based learning challenges many of the traditional practices of our schools:

- ◆ CBL suggests that instruction be designed to respond to specific student learning needs and support student progress toward clearly defined learning outcomes;
- ◆ The competency model requires a capacity for differentiation, allowing students to learn in different ways, and giving all the time needed for the development of proficiency for crucial skills;
- ◆ CBL requires the articulation of a clear sequence of learning objectives that lead to the desired outcomes and a plan for on-going assessment of progress.

In the competency model, students are not passed along with significant gaps in understanding that cause them to fall further and further behind. For the identified crucial learning outcomes, instruction is designed to match the developmental readiness of the students, so that they are engaged and challenged but not frustrated. Students advance upon mastery to higher levels of skill and challenge.

Competency based approaches are typically designed around five key elements (Sturgis, 2014):

1. Students advance upon mastery.
2. Competencies include explicit, measurable, transferable learning objectives that empower students.
3. Assessment is meaningful and a positive learning experience for students.
4. Students receive timely, differentiated support based on their individual learning needs.
5. Learning outcomes emphasize competencies that include application and creation of knowledge, along with the development of important skills and dispositions.

Personalized learning leading to competency is in evidence when a high-quality piano teacher carefully observes her student, challenges her to improve by giving her the assignment to learn a beautiful piece of music which is within her ability range, offers timely but not overwhelming suggestions for pacing and hand position, and gives her all the time needed to learn the music and be ready for a successful performance.

Learning is personalized when a computer tech student who studies for a test and comes up short is given immediate feedback on the answers that were incorrect and the opportunity to study some more and take the test again as soon as he is ready.

Personalized learning is built into the structure of quality digital math and reading programs. A clearly defined sequence of skills leads to competency. Essential steps in the sequence cannot be hurried through or avoided. At each step in the sequence of skills, competency must be demonstrated, and then a student moves forward to the next tier of instruction. The Khan Academy is a well-designed example of this structure, which is built with competency as the goal for each student.

A preschool to Grade 3 competency based math system (Sornson, 2014) identifies a competency framework for the early childhood years, including a small set of target math outcomes for each grade. Teachers are encouraged to offer a rich and interesting curriculum filled with activities and projects, while carefully monitoring progress toward this set of crucial outcomes. Some children may need to work on skills from the previous grade level. Others will be working at grade level, and still others will be working on skills from a more advanced level. Proficiency for each crucial skill will only be noted when a student has demonstrated deep understanding, over a period of time, using a variety of learning materials to ensure both understanding and application.

A personalized graduate school program identifies the crucial minimum skills and levels for competency in your field of study, assesses student skill levels, with the help of a mentor designs plans for learning which can include courses, work experiences, independent learning experiences, on-line courses, apprenticeships and other experiences, and then carefully monitors progress toward competency. Some students progress faster than others, and only when competency has been demonstrated for each crucial outcome is the degree awarded.

Personalized learning is in evidence on the job as employees work to attain new skills, are given both written and real life assessments, and develop a personal portfolio of skills that are valuable to the employer and offer opportunities for advancement.

A competency structure values learning over seat time. Accumulated Carnegie units or CEUs are not the coin of the realm in a competency based learning model. Rather, deep learning and the capacity to apply information and skills are the valued outcomes of competency based learning. A competency structure gives students the time they need to develop a crucial skill or concept. Six weeks may not be enough for some. Other students may be ready to move on more quickly. Lack of competency after the specified time for a course is not a life sentence. Within a competency model of instruction, critical skills are given the necessary time to develop.

A competency based system is designed to help every student become proficient in clearly defined essential outcomes and each of the steps leading to those outcomes. Instruction is designed so that students are in their optimal developmental zone, so that they are challenged but not pushed into frustration and disengagement. In a competency based learning system, students are not passed along from grade to grade with significant gaps in understanding, skill, and application.

> In a proficiency system, failure or poor performance may be part of the student's learning curve, but it is not an outcome.
>
> —Proficiency-Based Instruction and Assessment (Oregon Education Roundtable, 2009)

Crucial learning outcomes warrant personalized competency based learning. When coverage, enrichment, exposure, or an overview are not enough, competency based learning provides the path to achieving these outcomes. We want our children to develop competency before getting a driver's license because basic driving skills are crucial to their survival. Doctors, astronauts, electricians, and computer techs go through a competency based learning program to ensure that every essential skill has been fully developed so that they have the expertise needed for success.

Competency based learning works best when there are clearly defined learning objectives, a step-by-step plan for developing those skills, a careful assessment of the learner's skills and readiness, instruction at the student's developmental level, continued monitoring of progress, and instruction adjusted to her changing levels of skill until competency is achieved.

Every parent teaching his or her child to ride a bike knows how to design a personalized learning program leading to competency. It may take a year of practice before the training wheels come off. There may be a prolonged period in which you run alongside the bike to steady it as needed. There may even be a bump or bruise along the way, but with patience, your child learns to ride independently with confidence and skill.

10

Principles of Instruction Leading to Competency

The implementation of competency based learning relies on our ability to build a new model for instruction and learning, built upon principles that are substantially different than those of the industrial design of the curriculum-driven model. In this chapter, we consider six principles for instruction leading to competency.

Principles of Instruction Leading to Competency

1. Identify a manageable set of crucial outcomes to be the focus of on-going assessment.
2. Assess the learning needs of your students to determine skill levels and readiness for instruction.
3. Develop an instructional plan (curriculum) that allows you to teach a rich and interesting course of study while regularly monitoring progress toward essential outcomes.
4. Deliver instruction to match the learning needs of your students. Move proficient students on to more challenging learning opportunities, give developing students.

time to fully develop essential outcomes, and offer intensive support to students who need it.

5. Monitor progress toward essential outcomes consistently throughout the instructional process and adapt the level of difficulty so that students are challenged but never overwhelmed.

6. Do not compromise the standards of proficiency for an essential skill. These skills are crucial for success and deserve all the time needed for the development of competence.

Identify a Manageable Set of Crucial Outcomes to Be the Focus of On-Going Assessment

Begin with the end in mind, identify crucial learning outcomes, and establish clear milestones for progress so it is possible to monitor progress toward annual and long-term learning goals. Rather than giving teachers the mandate to "cover" a set of overwhelming content expectations, competency based learning must establish clear learning outcomes so that every teacher and every student knows exactly what is expected and needed for success. These crucial outcomes must be both clear and concise, establishing a framework of skills and knowledge that can be assessed by giving students multiple means and opportunities to demonstrate mastery through performance-based and other assessments.

Assess the Learning Needs of Your Students to Determine Skill Levels and Readiness for Instruction

Rather than asking, "What was covered in the previous grade?" the competency based teacher assesses what students know and what they are ready to learn. If content was covered but not learned, developing deep understanding of more complex content will be difficult or impossible until fundamental skills are learned. If students already have deep understanding of the prescribed grade level content, they are ready to advance to higher levels of learning.

Develop an Instructional Plan (Curriculum) that Allows You to Teach a Rich and Interesting Course of Study While Regularly Monitoring Progress Toward Essential Outcomes

Competency based instruction can enhance a love of learning and introduce students to new ideas and ways to learn. A quality course of study includes activities, projects, and opportunities to extend and integrate learning. Schools may wish to use curriculum maps and/or pacing guides to create an overall framework for instruction in the school. And within that instructional framework, there will be time for each student to develop crucial skills on the pathway to important academic and social-emotional outcomes.

Deliver Instruction to Match the Learning Needs of Your Students. Move Proficient Students on to More Challenging Learning Opportunities, Give Developing Students Time to Fully Develop Essential Outcomes, and Offer Intensive Support to Students Who Need It

Some instruction can be delivered as an introduction, overview, or even "coverage" of content. But essential outcomes will be held to the highest standard. Students learn best when offered instruction or learning opportunities that are a little bit challenging but not so difficult as to cause consistent failure, frustration, or disengagement. Crucial instruction will be designed to fit the needs of students and delivered in their instructional zone. This approach increases motivation to learn, time on task, and improves learning outcomes.

Monitor Progress toward Essential Outcomes Consistently throughout the Instructional Process, and Adapt the Level of Difficulty so that Students Are Challenged but Never Overwhelmed

As student skill levels improve, crucial instruction is adapted to meet the readiness levels of each student. Teachers carefully monitor progress through performance-based, observational, and other assessments to know when to give students more time and when to accelerate learning.

Do Not Compromise the Standards of Proficiency for an Essential Skill. These Skills Are Crucial for Success and Deserve all the Time Needed for the Development of Competence

Competency is demonstrated by learning content or a skill so well that it would be difficult to unlearn, so that you can use it in everyday life and apply it in multiple circumstances.

A competency based learning system is designed to enhance learning outcomes for our students but also to give teachers a much better chance to succeed. In recent decades, US education has taken a public relations beating. No longer does the United States have the preeminent educational system in the world. No longer do we have the best-educated workforce in the world.

Having worked in public education for many years, it is my observation that teachers and principals are among the most caring and hardest working people around (with only a few exceptions). As long as we hold onto the CTS model of instruction, the bad rap we get is likely to continue. We could work harder, teach more closely to the test, and put even more pressure on students, but Cover Test Sort is a model that is not designed to help a large majority of students become proficient learners.

We will continue to make small ineffectual gains at best until we fundamentally restructure our instructional process. Only a system designed to build competency will develop more competent learners. Only when we replace CTS with instruction leading to competency will we have significantly more students achieving at high levels, along with developing the qualities of character and the love of learning that are crucial for their futures.

Without a new model for teaching and learning, essential content and skills are likely to be "covered" but not well learned. With competency based learning, teachers vigilantly monitor learning and adjust instruction until each student develops essential understandings and skills to competency. With competency based learning, students travel the path toward essential learning outcomes at their own pace.

11

Teaching Differently

"It's my job to deliver the content. It's the students' job to keep up," a high school social studies teacher once explained to me. As a beginning high school special education teacher, his words told me all I needed to know: that I should never place another of our handicapped learners in his class and that many other students would suffer under his instruction. While this view is incredibly insensitive to the needs of students, it is also consistent with the structure of most curriculum-driven instructional systems. Teachers are given a lot to cover, told that they should be able to use their time well, cover every chapter and content expectation, manage behavior, and somehow motivate kids to try harder so they achieve higher test scores.

Imagine a school bus driver given a route to drive that is longer than could be reasonably managed in the time allowed. In this metaphor, drivers who race through the bus route and get to school on time are given kudos. And if you arrive at school with only a handful of kids, nobody complains.

When covering content is the prime objective, other behaviors suffer: taking time to build relationships, teaching and practicing classroom routines, helping kids get to know and trust each other, exploring each student's special interests, creating projects and activities that bring learning to life, developing intrinsic motivation to learn, and developing values and character.

Many new teachers have been trained to efficiently deliver content and lessons. When they reach the classroom, they confront the reality of behavior management, absenteeism, different learning skills, interests, and rates of learning, and the futility of "covering content" when students are not learning. These issues, along with complex school bureaucracies and a lack of professionalism in many school cultures, drives some of our best young educators away from teaching.

For those educators who have chosen to stay, the pressure to cover and the pressure to achieve better test scores has increased year by year. Because Cover Test and Sort is such a pervasive model, many educators don't even consider the alternatives. As we transition to competency based learning, the basic training we provide to teachers will change, on-going professional development will be important, and we will bring a much needed love of learning back into the schools and into our lives as professionals.

Learning to become a competency based educator is and will be a challenge. Instead of having one set of lessons to cover, the teacher will understand and respond to the diverse learning needs of her students. Instead of keeping all students on the same page at the same time, students work at their level of readiness. Instead of assuming all students learn in the same way, we recognize the many different ways in which competency might be achieved.

The rubric for high-quality instruction will change. No longer will the standard include:

- ◆ Lesson plans are consistent with the pacing guide and the prescribed GLCEs for each day.
- ◆ All students are receiving the prescribed and scripted lesson.
- ◆ Complete lessons are delivered in the 55-minute period.

Instead the rubric for high-quality instruction may include:

- ◆ Students are working toward essential outcomes at their own instructional level.
- ◆ Each student can identify the learning outcomes toward which he/she is working.
- ◆ Students understand what competency for each essential outcome will look like and how it can be demonstrated.
- ◆ Students seek help and support from each other, as well as from the teacher.
- ◆ The classroom is calm, and the students have developed a trusting relationship with teacher and classmates.
- ◆ The teacher effectively uses formative assessment to adjust instructional plans for each student.
- ◆ The teacher ensures that each student achieves true competency in every essential skill or step in a learning sequence.

At the secondary level, competency based learning can take many forms. Within a course-based competency framework, specific competencies for the completion of each course would be clearly defined. Students might test out of some of the specific competencies for each course, use blended learning options, gain experience or skill on the job, or show demonstrations of competency based on summer learning or work experiences.

A competency framework could be based on major areas of study rather than specific courses. These might include science, math, language arts, social science, technology, physical development, and the arts. In some schools, character development could be included as an expected aspect of development. Minimum standards for graduation/completion would be established, much like the New Hampshire K-12 Science Competencies (2014). Schools, working with students and families, might use varied options for learning to help students meet and exceed these standards.

To work within these competency based learning frameworks, the concept of high school itself may shift away from the identification of a place of learning to the experience of learning, wherever it may occur. Learning may shift away from curriculum silos (English, social studies, science, math) and will certainly shift away from the time-limited systems we currently use.

A competency based elementary program will focus on building all the important learning skills and habits that build the foundation of learning for life. New paradigms require different teaching methodologies and skills. Rather than using rigid one-size-fits-all pacing guides for essential learning outcomes, students are given instruction at their level. Group work is still appropriate for exploration and enrichment, and for projects and activities. Blended learning structures will develop, combining digital and in-person learning, but the importance of using high-quality educators to design instructional plans and to deliver crucial learning experiences will be preserved.

Using a competency based elementary learning system will open up new possibilities for parent involvement in the progress of their children. Parents and teachers working together can give children the practice time needed for proper skill development and accelerate progress on the pathways to high-level skill development.

In a competency based elementary classroom, there could be a small but clear set of crucial learning outcomes for each grade/age level. The importance of building a safe learning environment, teaching social skills and self-regulation through clear classroom and school procedures, and building a community of learners will be a priority.

Some portion of learning time may be filled with whole group instruction, activities, or projects. Using on-going assessments of progress, teachers will know exactly which children have achieved proficiency in the continuum of essential oral language, literacy, social skills, motor skills, numeracy, behavior, and self-regulation skills.

Some children may still be working on skills from the previous grade level. Others will be working at grade-level, and still others will be working on skills from a more advanced level. Proficiency in a skill will only be noted when a student has demonstrated deep understanding of a skill or concept on several occasions, over a period of time, and using several different types of learning materials to ensure both understanding and application.

Blended learning options will continue to increase and improve, as technology systems and learning programs are further improved. A deeper understanding of the content and skills that require social interaction, human language interaction, and/or the use of manipulatives will be developed, as content learning options are digitized.

Simpson County School District in rural Mississippi began implementation of a competency based early learning structure in 2008–09. Using the *Essential Skill Inventories* (Sornson, 2012a) in kindergarten, first, and second grade, staff learned to:

  ◆ Clearly identify essential learning outcomes in all the domains of early childhood;
  ◆ Use systematic assessment to determine the readiness levels of students in relation to essential outcomes;
  ◆ Offer informed instruction and carefully monitor progress until these skills/objectives are deeply understood (competency);
  ◆ Allow students to move on to more advanced learning as soon as they are ready.

The district aligned report cards with the *Essential Skill Inventories*, which encouraged staff to help parents understand the concept of crucial learning outcomes and to understand the competencies students were being asked to develop.

As part of an evaluation of improved teacher behaviors based on the use of this competency based learning model, teachers reported significant improvements in their teaching skills and behaviors associated with early learning success (Sornson, 2015). They reported improvement in systematic formative assessment, with the largest gain reported in their ability to embed assessment into the design of instruction. They described significant improvements in their skills for instructional design, with the largest gains reported in giving some students more time to learn essential skills and re-teaching essential skills until students reached deep understanding. Teachers described significant improvements in their skills and behaviors supporting differentiated instruction, and also significant improvements in their ability to understand the learning needs of the whole child.

Teacher perception of changes in their skills and behaviors is supported by changes in student outcomes at Simpson Central School, the pilot school that was the first Mississippi school to begin implementation. Both math and language arts scores have improved significantly on state assessments, and this school has risen from low performing to an A-rated school of excellence.

Competency based instruction is different than Cover Test and Sort. It offers a different contextual framework for planning and delivering instruction, which will require a different set of teaching skills.

University and technical competency based learning options are already beginning to proliferate. Employers are clamoring for applicants with the skills needed for success on the job, and higher education is responding. On-line and blended options are widely available. The availability of free Massive Open Online Courses (MOOCs) and other digital learning options add energy to this change. Around the world, nations have begun the transformation to a more efficient and personalized system of adult learning.

School to work programs, technical certificate programs, and degree programs recognize the need to have outcomes that matter and are reshaping their learning options. Competency based learning could be designed within a course-based framework, in which specific competencies for the completion of each course would be clearly defined. Or a degree program might define exit outcomes, assess student needs, and design a learning plan that helps students develop the required competencies. Students might test out of some of the specific competencies for each course or program, use blended learning options, gain experience or skill on the job, or show demonstrations of competency based on summer learning or work experiences. The pace of learning can vary, with some students more quickly moving along the skill pathways that lead to crucial exit outcomes.

High-quality CBL Teachers Will

♦ Use formative and summative assessment to understand the learning skills and needs of each student;
♦ Work unrushed within a viable curriculum;
♦ Teach crucial skills at the student's level of readiness;
♦ Differentiate instruction based on student learning needs;
♦ Use systematic formative assessment to monitor progress;
♦ Refine instruction as students show progress;
♦ Consider blended learning options;
♦ Develop working relationships with students and parents;
♦ Support instruction/learning until crucial skills and content are fully proficient.

No amount of tweaking to the assembly line CTS model will adequately meet the learning needs of our future. The competency based teacher will be a well-trained and highly skilled professional educator, able to identify crucial outcomes, assess student learning needs, and differentiate instruction towards the development of competency. We are stepping into a new age, in which educators will be valued professionals, helping lead our students to the learning skills needed to be successful men and women in the modern world.

12

Identifying Crucial Outcomes

It all starts with clear learning goals. A system that is designed primarily around "coverage" does not give the attention to crucial learning outcomes that a competency based learning model produces. With a small set of clearly defined crucial outcomes, or a clear pathway to competency, and a goal of competency for every child, teachers work within a different system designed to produce far more competent learners.

Thoughtful educators have been calling for a clearer and narrower instructional focus for decades.

"Students learn more when we teach less—but teach it well" (Dempster, 1993).

"The tendency toward overload is strong in schools—and crippling to improvement efforts" (Fullan & Hargreaves, 1996).

Although US mathematics textbooks attempt to address 175 percent more topics than do German textbooks and 350 percent more topics than do Japanese textbooks, both German and Japanese students significantly outperform US students in mathematics. Similarly, although US science textbooks attempt to cover 930 percent more topics than do German textbooks and

433 percent more topics than do Japanese textbooks, both German and Japanese students significantly outperform US students in science achievement as well (Schmidt, McKnight, & Raizen, 1996).

We will realize the promise of school reform when we establish standards and expectations for reaching them that are clear, not confusing; essential, not exhaustive. The result will be a new coherence and a shared focus that could be the most propitious step we can take toward educating all students well (Schmoker & Marzano, 1999).

The National Mathematics Advisory Council recommends that math curriculum should include fewer topics, spending enough time to make sure each is learned in enough depth that it need not be revisited in later grades (National Mathematics Advisory Council, 2008).

The Professional Learning Community (PLC) model developed by Rick DuFour, Bob Eaker, and Becky DuFour (2008) focuses on four critical questions:

- ◆ What do we expect students to learn?
- ◆ How do we know when they have learned it?
- ◆ How will we respond when students don't learn?
- ◆ How will we respond when students have learned?

At the conclusion of his work *Visible Learning* (2009), John Hattie synthesized hundreds of educational research studies over several decades and concluded that the most powerful strategy for improving student learning occurs when teachers work together in collaborative teams to collectively complete the following tasks:

- ◆ Clarify what student must learn;
- ◆ Gather evidence of student learning;
- ◆ Analyze evidence of student learning;
- ◆ Identify the most effective teaching strategies.

It all starts with clear learning goals. With a small set of clearly defined crucial outcomes, a clear pathway to competency, and a goal of competency for every child, teachers work within a different system designed to produce far more competent learners. Clear learning goals provide the objective toward which we will work until the job is done.

In the ever-growing and changing world of technology, Microsoft, Oracle, Cisco, Apple, Google, Ubuntu, and other providers offer professional certifications for those who complete training and demonstrate competency in a clearly articulated set of skill expectations. Each certification is specific to one set of skills. Advanced certifications rely on the development of a progression of skills sets, a pathway to higher-level skills. Only with competency in each required skill is a certificate earned.

Electricians are expected to show competency in a specific set of skills to be licensed as master electrician, journeyman electrician, residential wireman, maintenance electrician, or electrical contractor. These could be considered end-goal competencies, requirements for certification or employment.

In 2013, as part of its competency based learning initiative, the New Hampshire State Board of Education approved college- and career-ready competencies in mathematics and English language arts. With these end-goals in mind, educators must then build a careful sequence of learning steps for which competency is the standard.

Building a competency based pathway is different than developing curriculum maps or a sequence of grade level content expectations. Curriculum maps and GLCEs are descriptions of what will be covered and when. A competency pathway specifies the learning steps for which coverage is not enough, and for which we must allow time to be a variable, giving each student the support and time needed for full development of deep understanding and application. For the skills in a competency sequence, time is the variable, and proficiency is the expectation.

A competency pathway should not be viewed as a path to credit hours or Carnegie units, which rely on the time-limited and age-based CTS learning model. Instead, a competency pathway is focused on student learning outcomes and is built with the following design principles in mind:

- ♦ Students advance upon mastery, not age.
- ♦ The pathway is built with explicit and measurable learning objectives.
- ♦ Assessment is primarily formative, and skills or concepts are assessed in multiple contexts to guarantee both deep understanding and application.

Competency based pathways rely on a sequence of explicit learning goals, allowing students to work at the appropriate level of challenge and progress to the next level of challenge as soon as they are completely ready. Crucial learning goals can be stated as end-goals, but a competency based pathway is comprised of the many crucial learning goals that lead to a sought after end-goal.

Pathways to competency can take different forms. Medical school and Navy Seal training offer explicit end-goal competencies, and stages and skills in the development of those competencies, but with the clear expectation that not all candidates will complete the training.

The Khan Academy and other web-based learning platforms offer step-by-step strategies to higher-level outcomes. Students can take as much time as needed to work on each learning goal. When proficiency is achieved, the next goals become available to the learner.

A competency structure could include a set of crucial outcomes taught as a course. For some students, competency could be achieved by taking the course once. For other students, it might take more than one time to achieve competency in the required outcomes. Using this type of structure, in which some students are likely to take the course again, it would serve students better if only a small set of outcomes were taught as one unit, to avoid the need for students to repeat a whole semester or year of learning.

A high school biology class might include a competency structure in which a set of crucial outcomes is identified, and all students are expected to achieve proficiency in these outcomes. In addition to the basic competencies, there might be a set of higher-level competencies for some of the students in the class, which are not considered essential for course completion.

In a school-to-work design, local school leaders at the high school, community college, or technical school may have constructed a learning plan in cooperation with local employers. In addition to basic school requirements, students would have the opportunity to choose a course of study that leads to competency in a specific set of skills that are needed for jobs available in the community.

Essential Math Skills (Sornson, 2014) offers a competency based math structure for the preschool to Grade 3 years. It describes the 29 foundation skills that are essential for long-term math learning success. These are the skills that merit continued monitoring and development until they are completely proficient. A developmentally appropriate set of skills is identified for each age/grade level from Pre-K to Grade 3, which provides a competency framework for the classroom teacher. The *EMS* is not intended to be a complete math curriculum or program, which should be designed to include projects, activities, extensions, and a larger set of content to cover. But it does provide a specific learning sequence for teachers, along with 8–12 manipulative-based activities for teachers to use for the development of competency in each early math skill. In a competency based classroom, some students would be expected to be working on grade level, while others would be completing work from previous levels or advancing to the level typically associated with the next grade.

In Kennewick, Washington, as reported in *Annual Growth for All Students, Catch Up Growth for Those Who Are Behind* (Fielding, 2007), the school district identified a sequence of skill levels for the development of phonemic awareness, phonics, accuracy, fluency, and comprehension. Using a process of formative assessment, progress in these aspects of literacy development was carefully monitored, and students were then given instruction and practice time for each skill until it was mastered.

The Pre-K to Grade 3 Essential Skill Inventories (Sornson, 2012) are based on a competency based structure for each of the domains of early childhood. Progress on the crucial skills for oral language, phonological skills, literacy, numeracy, sensory-motor, behavior, and self-regulation skills are monitored systematically to ensure that each child is given the time and support needed for the development of proficiency in each skill of each domain.

Competency based learning frameworks require a different way of thinking about teaching and learning. Without the primary directive to "cover content" at the same rate for all students, we are faced with the challenge of defining specific learning pathways leading to competencies that matter.

13

Planning Instruction to Meet Students' Needs

Scripted and rigidly paced learning programs be warned. Your time is up. The coverage-driven learning model cannot be saved. Parents would never use this model to teach their children to catch a ball, or ride a bike, or drive a car. Soon they will realize it must not be used on their children for other crucial learning outcomes, like reading and writing, science and math.

In the CTS model of instruction, teachers are asked to skillfully construct lessons so that somehow every student is interested and engaged, despite the astounding variance in skill levels and learning readiness of their students. *Deliver a great lesson. Test the students. Give them grades (as a motivation to try harder). And move on to the next lesson.* For more than a century, working within this model, teachers have worried over the details of every lesson plan, hoping to somehow offer more successful learning experiences to their students.

But using this time-limited learning model has overwhelming limitations. Some students need more time to learn important content. Some students don't have the prerequisite skills and really need to step back and fill in the gaps of important learning sequences. Other students already know the material and are bored. Some students have been sick and out of school, and others have challenges outside of school and can't concentrate in the classroom.

Competency based learning is focused on student learning outcomes and is built with the following design principles in mind:

♦ Students advance upon mastery, not age;
♦ The pathway to competency is built with explicit and measurable learning objectives;
♦ Assessment is primarily formative, and skills or concepts are assessed in multiple contexts to guarantee both deep understanding and application.

The challenge and opportunity for schools and educators is to learn a new way of teaching that is far more effective for a greater number of students, to develop pathways to competencies needed for success in the information age, and to develop classroom and other learning systems in which students and teachers find success, respect, confidence, and joy.

Our work has just begun. A limited number of states are vigorously exploring competency based learning models, while in most states and school districts CBL is barely a rumor. And yet it is all around us. Our doctors, pilots, electricians, and tech advisors have experienced competency based learning systems with clearly defined learning outcomes and the requirement to demonstrate competency. Our gymnastics, martial arts, and scouting programs are built upon progress based on demonstrated competency.

It starts with the identification of crucial learning outcomes. These could be grade/age or course-specific, or they could be identified as part of a sequence of crucial steps on a pathway to long-term learning goals. These are the skills that merit continued monitoring and development until they are completely proficient.

Imagine teaching a high school biology class in which you have a rich and interesting curriculum but also a competency framework. A small set of crucial content and skill competencies have been identified, and teachers have learned to offer instruction and still have the ability to track each student's progress toward the essential outcomes. Because the curriculum is viable, teachers have time to **monitor progress and adjust instruction** for students who are struggling, as well as for those who are ready to move ahead. While whole class lecture, demonstration, projects, and activities are common, there is also regular attention given to small groups, digital learning system supports, peer tutoring, and other approaches to individualizing instruction.

Imagine a middle school math class, in which specific math skills have been identified as the crucial outcomes for sixth grade. Most of the class is ready to work on these skills but will progress at different rates. Some students are behind and lack deep understanding of skills going back to second grade. Other students are ahead and are ready for skills typically taught in seventh or eighth grade. In a competency based math learning system, the teacher will use formative assessment to understand the needs of each student within the structure of essential math skills. Demonstration, peer tutoring, blended learning, small group lessons, and digital resources like the Khan Academy are among the instructional options available to the teacher as she **monitors progress toward the crucial outcomes and plans instruction to meet the needs of her students.** On any given day, the teacher may offer a demonstration, work with two different small groups, supervise students who are working on Khan, and have two students who travel to another class to participate in higher-level instruction. Students spend significant minutes each day learning and practicing math at their level of readiness. Because students are experiencing success each day, motivation is good, and discipline problems are few. Group activities and class beginning and ending routines help create a positive community climate and contribute to language, social, and collaboration skills.

Imagine an elementary school in which both grade level crucial competencies and age-range pathways to competency have been established in all the domains of development, including language, literacy, numeracy, motor skills, social skills, and self-regulation skills. The curriculum map ensures "coverage" of key grade-level concepts, but coverage is not the end-goal.

Teachers are expected to know their students and vigilantly monitor progress toward crucial grade level outcomes. Teachers design instruction so that students are exposed to general concepts and also have time to develop essential skills at students' specific levels of readiness, whatever that might be. Instructional level, student interests, required curriculum, essential learning outcomes, and the social dynamic of each class are considered by the teacher as she designs instruction for each upcoming week. By knowing each student and offering big doses of learning at each level, student learning gains are optimized. By carefully monitoring progress, the teacher knows if progress has stalled in any learning domain. If so, she collaborates with colleagues and experiments with any factors that might be the critical piece to help this student get back on track. **Constantly monitoring, constantly adjusting instruction,** this teacher is a high-quality, high-skill professional.

Imagine a preschool in which the teacher has a high-quality curriculum framework and also monitors progress toward crucial kindergarten readiness skills in oral language, literacy, number sense, visual motor skills, gross motor skills, behavior, and self-care. Each week, she **monitors progress** in at least two of these domains of early childhood, and each week she **plans instruction based on a clear understanding of student learning needs.** As important as any learning outcome, the teacher builds a culture for connection and learning. Children are safe and happy; challenged but never overwhelmed.

Imagine a university that offers both certificates and degrees. Each certificate and each degree program has established minimum competencies for completion. For these knowledge and skill competencies, there are no grades. There is only competency. You can take a course or engage in a learning activity as many times as necessary to learn what you need to become competent. If you have already developed a competency on the job, in a previous course, or through independent learning, you are not asked to take courses to revisit that skill or content. Degree programs include more than a set of minimum competencies. They also include **a personal design for learning,** a set of skill and content outcomes that you have chosen as important to you, in combination with the minimum competencies expected for your degree. The university is then a partner in helping define learning pathways that will lead to the competencies that support your plan for your future.

> As we move toward a competency based learning framework, there are incredible opportunities for enterprising educators. New learning delivery systems that are not confined to the structure of a time-limited course and new assessment systems to track progress toward competency are already being devised.

The Khan Academy has developed a "Constellation of Math Skills," which displays the relationships between math skills, and from which a pathway from basic math to higher order skills can be inferred. In early math development, the *Essential Math Skills* (Sornson, 2014) shows a progression of crucial skills from preschool to grade three, along with many movement- and manipulative-based activities to develop each skill to deep understanding. Various digital math learning programs are built upon a progression of skills, which in digital format can be carefully tracked for progress toward competency.

In the crucial early childhood years (preschool through grade three), there are skills in oral language, reading, phonologic skills, writing, motor skills, numeracy, social, and self-regulation that are crucial for the experience of early learning success and, therefore, crucial to establish a healthy learning trajectory for life. Using a manageable set of crucial outcomes for these years, the *Essential Skill Inventories* (Sornson, 2012a) give teachers discrete learning outcomes for each grade but also a sequence of skills that allow each student to be given instruction at the right instructional level to maximize learning and avoid disengagement.

In New Hampshire, the State Board of Education has established college- and career-ready outcome standards for ELA, math, and science. Along with clear competency expectations for graduation, they have also developed a structure of recommended content and process standards for required high school coursework.

Digital learning programs like Luminosity develop cognitive skills including speed, memory, attention, problem solving (http://brain-games-puzzle-stores-review.toptenreviews.com/lumosity-review.html), and flexibility. The program carefully monitors progress and adjusts the rate of difficulty so that students are challenged but never frustrated to the point of disengagement. VINCI is an early childhood focused company whose game-based learning systems tracks progress, offers activities in the student's instructional zone, and gradually tiers instruction to higher levels of competency in language, math, and science.

Western Governor's University developed a self-paced, personalized, online learning program to meet the needs of adults who did not have the time or access to a traditional university experience. WGU has served as a model and a catalyst for the many universities now offering some version of competency based learning.

> The most important innovations in competency based learning will happen in classrooms and schools across the nation. Our work has just begun.

For most of us, with our personal experiences growing up in CTS schools, being trained using CTS standards, and working as educators within the typical CTS school structure, learning new skills for competency based learning will be a challenge. In a competency based system, it will be far more important that educators have well-developed skills for formative assessment, understanding the needs of the whole child, differentiated instruction, working with parents, developing a culture of personal responsibility for learning, and professional collaboration.

It is entirely possible for a teacher to "cover" a unit or chapter without carefully understanding the learning needs of his students. Some teachers find the coverage model comfortable and will resist changing to a model that requires more knowledge of each student and more ability to differentiate instruction. Helping teachers understand this new model for learning and develop skills to support high-quality competency based learning will take the steady leadership of administrators and teacher leaders. Developing initiatives to help teachers become "competent" in the skills to support CBE will require professional development and teacher assessment systems much different than those which are typical today.

High-quality competency based learning will depend on professional collaboration in schools. The complexity of understanding and responding to the needs of individual learners demands the benefits of teamwork. Developing new systems, procedures, conversations, and skills will take a learning community, a living model of the collaborative learning community we want for our students.

In a competency based learning system, administrators will have a different role and need different skills than in today's typical schools. Managing a CTS system includes enforcing pacing guides, providing security for state assessments, spending countless hours evaluating teachers, defending test scores to the public, working with unhappy parents, enforcing discipline with students who are frustrated or bored, and trying to find a few minutes to build relationships and provide instructional leadership.

In a competency based system, with its emphasis on personalized learning and clear outcomes, effective leaders will act as coaches, build professional learning groups, help develop pathways to competency for both students and staff, support differentiated instruction, develop the culture and climate for effective learning and teaching, and build professional routines that support the process of helping every child follow the pathways that lead to competency. The transition to competency will require leaders who can work with others, hold to a clear vision of a new learning model, continue to be open to learning, build networks of collaboration, and be the calm voice of change.

Disciplined innovation is an essential ingredient of successful teaching in a competency based learning system. With clear outcomes in mind, and with a careful awareness of the needs of each student, the competency based teacher develops a teaching/learning plan, implements, and then uses formative assessment to discover that it worked better for some students than for others. Some students need more time, and the disciplined innovator figures a way to give them more time. Some students develop proficiency in a skill far more quickly than expected, and the disciplined innovator moves those students forward to more challenging skills and content. Some students don't respond well at all to the instructional plan. It's a miss. Rather than blame those students, the disciplined teacher-innovator considers other ways to teach every crucial concept or skill. Whatever it takes. Any amount of time, in or out of school, in groups or on a screen, using paper or using manipulatives, the disciplined innovator finds a way to help students learn.

Helping each child progress on the path to clear learning goals requires disciplined, instructional innovation based on actionable data every single day.

Successful competency-focused educators will plan instruction with the understanding that, for every crucial outcome, competency takes precedence over coverage. Teachers will devise pathways to competency, carefully monitor progress, modify instruction to fit student readiness, and give students all the time needed to achieve learning success. Highly skilled professional educators, with an in-depth understanding of each student and with skills in formative assessment and differentiated instruction, will create classrooms and programs where learning comes alive.

14

Self-Regulation and Intrinsic Motivation

"Just tell us what's going to be on the test so we know what to study," is a common refrain in many schools.

In CTS schools, students are told what is worth learning. Content is delivered in a time-limited format. A test will determine how well they learned it. Some students are overwhelmed and confused by the content. Some students are incredibly bored. Some students don't have the underlying skills or knowledge needed to be highly successful in this subject no matter how hard they try. Some students disengage from learning and just show up, hoping that they might somehow magically pass the test and get a credit. For all of them it will be the same test. Then each student receives a grade. Then we move on.

In most schools, students are told what to learn and then extrinsically motivated by grades, credits, class rank, status, and admission to college. High-stakes testing has added pressure to the system, making pacing guides more rigid and district assessment schedules more aggressive. This system design is deeply troubling if you recognize the importance of self-initiated learning in the information age.

In a world where lifelong learning was a privilege to be enjoyed by only a few men and women, the CTS design worked well enough. Since we are now living in a world in which new information and new technology are constantly changing the demands of the workplace, the CTS design is doing incredible harm by causing many students to disengage and others to expect that learning should be easy.

Successful learners in the information age must be curious and excited about learning. Effective learners will have the habits of mind that allow them to gather information, pose clear theories, investigate, persist, collaborate, critically review, and change ideas based on new information. In the other-directed learning environment of a Cover Test and Sort school, the emphasis is far more on compliance and completion than on self-regulation and intrinsic motivation to learn.

The importance of self-regulation for successful lifelong learning can hardly be overstated. Self-regulation begins with the development of self-calming, focusing, persisting, delaying gratification, and adjusting your emotional, physical, and attentional state to meet the needs of your situation. As students develop basic self-regulation skills, they become calm enough on the inside to look outside of themselves and notice the lives and feelings of others. This is empathy, which is a foundation for the development of social skills and social-emotional intelligence. The capacity to self-regulate for both social and academic learning is among the best predictors of who will become successful in school, in work, and in life.

A three-decade-long study in New Zealand (Moffitt et al., 2011) looking at more than 1,000 young people showed that children with low self-regulation are:

- ♦ More likely to smoke, have health problems, and have bad credit;
- ♦ Three times more likely to commit a crime;
- ♦ Three times more likely to have multiple addictions;
- ♦ Two times more likely to be single parents.

As reported by Angela Duckworth and others (2007), self-regulation contributes to the development of resilience and character. In Walter Mischel's famous Marshmallow Experiment, a researcher offered four-year-old children a marshmallow. The researcher offered each child a choice. On the desk was a bell. She was going to leave the room, and the child could ring the bell at any time and eat one marshmallow on her return. But if the child waited for the researcher to return on her own after 15 minutes, the child would get two marshmallows instead of one.

Mischel and colleagues (1989) tracked the academic progress of these students over time, and the correlation between the child's wait time and later academic success was significant. Many years after, children who waited for fifteen minutes had SAT scores that were on average 210 points higher than those of children who rang the bell after only thirty seconds. The capacity to self-regulate, whether by an ability to distract themselves or delay gratification, had contributed to the development of the learning skills measured on this college entry exam.

> In a well-devised competency based learning system, self-regulation and intrinsic motivation to learn will be among the crucial outcomes to help students become successful lifelong learners.

In a competency based learning system, students will clearly understand their learning goals and have models of what successful completion looks like. Teachers will adjust the difficulty of instruction to match the student's readiness for every crucial learning outcome so that each child has the opportunity to give effort and achieve success. Each child will get the time needed for achievement of proficiency. No shortcuts will be taken that leave students with gaps in the development of crucial skills or concepts. Effort will be encouraged. Students will consistently experience the connection between engagement and effort with successful learning. Motivation for learning will be enhanced by the experience of success.

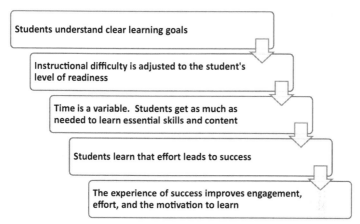

FIGURE 14.1   Competency Based Learning and Motivation

In classrooms across America today, there are students who are frustrated, and others who are bored. The frustrated kids try, fail, and begin to shut down. They learn that effort and persistence are not enough, and they become disengaged learners who seldom practice using focus, persistence, inquiry, or reflection in the classroom.

The bored kids know that they can pass most tests with minimal effort, so they tune out. Someone else chose a set of learning outcomes that seem unconnected to each other or to life. Without much challenge, without any personal connection to the material, and without clear goals to reach, the process of learning is dull. They tune out, ask questions like "What do I have to study to pass this test?" or "What do I need to get a B?"

In a competency based learning system (Figure 14.1), far more students will develop patterns of self-initiated learning, pursing clear learning goals, making progress on pathways to competency at their own pace, and choosing additional content for exploration, enrichment, or pure learning pleasure. Students will understand that effort and application bring learning rewards, embrace the challenge, and choose to learn.

With clear and meaningful learning goals, instead of avoiding learning, more students will embrace learning. At home, on weekends, in the summer, we will see students choose to make progress on the pathways that lead to important outcome competencies. Any time, any place, any pace learning is the responsibility of schools, families, and individuals in a competency driven learning system.

The lack of joyful self-initiated learning builds patterns of disengagement and lassitude. The capacity to self-regulate and learn to work hard, focus sharply, and persist to reach exciting learning outcomes is crucial for modern learners. As we design competency based learning systems, it will be important to focus not just on the development of academic and technical skills but to also include skills that help students take ownership of their own success, including self-regulation, empathy, intrinsic motivation, and social-emotional skills.

15

Building a Positive Environment for Learning

If our goal is to help far more students become successful learners for life, we must build classrooms and other learning environments in which students are calm, focused, self-regulated, and ready to learn. During the last few decades, however, in many schools we've moved further away from the careful development of safety, trust, and relationships as part of classroom management.

"I used to take time to build connections with my students," many teachers have explained to me, "but there is just not time for that anymore." In the rush to cover more content and do more test-prep, teachers have done what they felt they must. Time to get to know each student, help students get to know the teacher, carefully teach classroom procedures, practice procedures until they become routines, and help students get to know and trust each other has been surrendered to the district pacing guides.

A CTS instructional system values "coverage" as its top priority. Pacing guides, district assessments, long lists of standards, curriculum maps, state testing, and teacher evaluation systems in sum convey a clear message: deliver the content.

It has been incorrectly assumed within the CTS model that rigorous coverage leads to better testing outcomes. In fact, since the early 1970s, all the pressure to increase both content coverage and assessment has not resulted in any significant gains in learning outcomes for American high school students as demonstrated on the National Assessment of Educational Progress (National Center for Education Statistics, 2015). But even without any evidence that an accelerated "coverage" system works, we have largely continued to perseverate on its use.

Within the coverage-driven classroom, compliant students help create the opportunity to cover more content. Disruptive student behaviors are unwelcome and quickly discouraged using a variety of behavior management techniques. But compliant students are not necessarily listening, engaged, curious, or learning. Within the coverage-driven classroom, tuning out or disengagement, as long as it does not disrupt others, tends to be tolerated.

Under the guise of coverage-driven rigor, many classrooms have become unsafe environments for students, places where:

- ◆ Students compete with each other for better grades rather than collaborate in support of one another;
- ◆ Students might be ridiculed by other students or by the teacher;
- ◆ Attention is given to the things you do wrong;
- ◆ Your mistakes are called to the attention of others;
- ◆ Your weaker skills are easily exposed;
- ◆ Student misbehavior is tolerated rather than taking the time to deal with it effectively;
- ◆ There is little time available for building positive social skills, emotional intelligence, or relationships with others.

In the pursuit of better testing outcomes, schools have chosen rigorous curriculum expectations over the importance of classroom culture, relationships, trust, play, character building, and social-emotional learning. It's ironic because we have neglected the conditions for learning that might lead to better testing outcomes.

Highly anxious or insecure students don't learn well, and our present CTS system is creating anxiety for our kids at a record pace. But it's not just affecting the kids. We might also reflect on how the CTS model is not serving our educators. According to the MetLife Annual Survey of Teachers (2013), more than half (51 percent) of teachers report experiencing great stress almost every day. Teacher satisfaction has continued to decline, with only 39 percent reporting being very satisfied with their jobs in 2012.

As we move to competency based learning models, we have the opportunity to build classrooms and learning programs that are much more respectful and joyful, and which also help to produce better learning results for more students. The deliberate planning of safe, secure, trusting classroom and school cultures will not only benefit the learning rates of children. We should also consider the school culture and its impact on staff as we begin our transition into competency based learning. If we expect educators to be engaged in continuous professional learning and thoughtful problem solving, school culture matters.

For our students, it starts with trust and relationships. Is the class well managed? Will I be safe here? Will people hurt or humiliate me? Will I be successful?

With security established in the learning environment, educators have a chance to help students develop crucial self-regulation skills. These include the ability to calm yourself, focus, persist, delay gratification, and adjust yourself to meet the needs of your situation. Children with the capacity for self-regulation can get loud and excited when playing outside, then calm and focused when it's time to get to work.

With self-regulation comes the internal control to be calm enough on the inside to begin to pay careful attention to what is going on in the lives of others. Moving beyond self-absorption allows for the development of empathy, which is the foundation for all social skills and emotional intelligence. The ability to notice and understand others helps us learn to work with others effectively, to be a good playmate or team member, and can lead to the capacity for collaboration in the workplace and in life.

Self-regulation also enables students to act more confidently and successfully in the world, take on challenges, and try new things. Self-regulation allows for the development of grit, stick-to-itiveness, resilience, and courage.

A student who feels safe, is able to be calm and focused, can persist and delay gratification, and adjusts himself to meet the needs of any situation is far more likely to be successful in school and in life. With this pattern well-developed, the student is more able to develop empathy, resilience, social skills, and emotional intelligence.

Thoughtful teachers have long understood the importance of classroom culture. They take the time to get to know your students; allow students to get to know them; build a predictable and secure classroom culture; develop classroom routines that help every student learn the behaviors that lead to success; practice these routines until they are consistently used by every student; and create opportunities for students to build relationships with each other. With a positive classroom culture in place, students are more likely to feel safe, be secure that in this place no one will hurt or embarrass them, stay engaged, be respectful of others, and make efforts to learn.

In a competency based learning system, we begin by identifying crucial outcomes. Self-regulation, empathy, emotional intelligence, and character matter. In a competency based learning environment, educators and parents will work together to help students develop social-emotional competencies, which are as important as any academic learning outcome.

16

Creating a Learning Organizational Culture

Imagine the daunting learning tasks in front of us.

A university department, which has been accredited largely based on what gets covered within each degree program, and which for years has argued about the details of every course syllabus and curriculum plan, begins to move toward a competency based learning approach. Instead of measuring the number of credit hours in which a student has earned a "C" or better, the faculty begins to design a competency based structure in which each degree or certificate has a set of essential learning outcomes along with student-directed learning outcomes. Not only that, but now students can use previous life experiences and out-of-school experiences to develop proficiency in these outcomes as part of their degree program. Without competency, students do not earn the degree. After demonstrating competency in every essential (content and/or skill) learning outcome, along with additional student-directed learning goals, she earns the degree or certificate.

The department goes to work, establishing a competency framework that matches present and future needs for skills and knowledge in each degree and certificate program. They clearly define each competency and consider a process through which students can develop a plan to demonstrate a competency. Staff works collaboratively to develop a process that allows student

individual learning goals to be part of each student's comprehensive instructional plan. Courses are revised to match the
learning needs of students working within this model. Some
courses are broken up into modules that can be used to match
specific student learning needs. Apprenticeships, internships,
online learning options, and a host of other ways to learn are
considered and cataloged as options to consider within the development of a plan that meets the needs of a student and also
holds to a high standard for learning outcomes.

A high school begins to experiment with competency based
programming. At first, they take some easy steps. Participation
in sports can be used to earn a required credit in Physical Education. A co-op or internship position can be used for credit if
the responsibilities match up to the expectations for a math,
business, or social studies course. Online learning options outside of the school day are considered for credit, and testing-out
opportunities for some required courses are made available. In
these cases, the basic system of course and credit requirements
has been maintained.

This high school staff and the school board decide to go
further. They begin the process of looking at each course and
considering what learning outcomes are essential for a student's
graduation and, more importantly, for success in life. The grading structure is called into question. No longer can you pass
with a C. Students can complete a course as soon as they have
demonstrated competency in all essential outcomes for a course.
Students can also take a course as many times as needed to
achieve competency in any of the identified essential
outcomes.

A myriad of options and questions emerge. How will the
school define clear criteria for competency so that all staff holds
to the same standards? How do we include student and parent
input in the design of a learning plan? At what point do we
forget about credits and grades and simply work toward the
defined competencies we have established as a baseline for
graduation? Some students have gaps in understanding basic
level (second/third grade) math skills. Can the school structure
learning opportunities that meet these and other similar learning

needs? What are the steps that lead to the development of graduation-level outcomes, and how do we help students develop absolute competency for each step along the path to those outcomes? Can we certify students in skills that go beyond the skills that are required for high school graduation? Can we collaborate with local businesses to build competency profiles that match the needs of local employers and keep jobs and companies in the community? How do we maintain an emphasis on developing a well-rounded student and maintain instruction designed to explore and extend knowledge?

At a middle school, recognizing the diverse learning needs among their students, educators decide to skip over the stage of aligning competencies with courses. They identify core middle school completion competencies and pathways to achieving these competencies. Included among their core competencies are social-emotional skills and self-regulatory skills. They develop data tracking systems to follow the progress of each student. Because so many of the crucial competencies overlap between disciplines, science and math instructors look for ways to work together. Project-based and activity-based learning is used to challenge students and allow them to work at the optimal level of challenge for themselves. Collaboration is encouraged. Home learning, summer learning, experience-based learning, blended learning, and other options are explored. Report cards are an analysis of progress toward the middle school core competencies.

At a state department of education, officials recognize the ridiculous nature of the Continuing Education Unit (CEU) system we've historically used for maintaining professional certificates. One CEU equals ten contact hours. If you are present and remember to sign in and sign out, you earn your contact hours. During training hours, some teachers are playing on their phones. Others may be drifting off into out-of-body experiences. The learning needs of the educators are not assessed in this process. The quality of instruction is not considered. Learning outcomes are not considered. CEUs are all about seat time and have never equated to learning or to teaching skills.

The department of education begins the process of change. A careful review of the measurable skills needed for entry-level and tenured teachers are considered. A framework for the steps to competency is established. The role of teacher training institutions, professional associations, and school districts for the basic, remedial, and advanced training needs of educators is discussed. If we want the best teachers, we must have a plan for professional learning that leads to skills that matter.

At an elementary school, educators make a commitment to helping every child build a solid foundation of basic skills by the end of third grade and then to refine these skills with an emphasis on intrinsic motivation to learn and personal habits of learning. These educators choose a competency based framework for all the domains of early childhood (*Essential Skills Inventory, Preschool through Grade 3*, Sornson, 2012a), and they identify core upper-elementary competencies that integrate with the middle school core competencies. Report cards are aligned with the competencies and serve as a way to deepen discussions with parents regarding the developmental process and the development of the whole child.

With a long history of covering lessons and moving along with the pacing guide, teachers must relearn basic planning and instructional practices. The habit of teaching without careful regard for student readiness is hard to break. Teachers are challenged to be consistent as they collect high-quality observational data. Improved data leads to improved differentiated instruction, and teachers begin to collaborate more to share ideas about both embedded assessment and informed differentiated instruction. As they know students better, especially in social-emotional, language, and sensory-motor domains, staff find themselves more deeply understanding the connections between domains and building better relationships with students.

At a preschool, the staff has always been tuned into the development of the whole child but now begins to use a competency framework that helps them define crucial outcomes in each domain. Activity within a domain is not confused with competency. Teachers are able to recognize any gaps in development and also when to accelerate instruction to meet the needs of each child.

Because preschool teachers are always busy, it can be challenging to develop the habits of systematically monitoring progress in each of the early childhood domains. For some teachers, it is difficult to learn to embed assessment into the process of instruction; somehow, assessment has been connected to one-on-one time away from instruction. But now the staff is learning to assess student learning while kids are engaged in the natural process of learning. For some, it is hard to trust their own observations and to assume that parents and administrators will give validity to the data that is based on their observations. Clear systems for on-going assessment must be developed.

Teachers learn to assess one skill using several different learning situations, materials, or formats. Teachers learn that quality observational assessment, judgments based on careful scrutiny, using specific rubrics, over several days, using multiple learning situations is far more reliable than any snap-shot one day paper-and-pencil assessment. They learn to share strategies for both assessment and instruction. Professional respect is enhanced, and collaboration becomes the norm rather than the exception.

Creating a Learning Culture

One assumption used in each of the above descriptions is that adult educators have the capacity to work together and learn together in collaborative groups. For this to occur, competency based schools will need to work to create the conditions for high-quality adult learning.

Like children, in fact like all humans, we learn better and collaborate better when we work within a culture of trust, safety, positive communication, and personal connection. But the top-down authoritarian design of Taylor and the historic use of separate classrooms for delivering instruction have not contributed to the development of collaborative cultures in our schools. In the same way that a thoughtful classroom teacher takes the time to develop a positive classroom culture, teacher leaders and administrative leaders look for ways to enhance connection, build trust, build awareness, create teams, grow human capacity, build habits of continuous learning, and learn to be collaborative learning teams. Creating the conditions for great learning and collaboration becomes a priority in a competency based learning environment.

For decades, state and district education officials have set the expectations for what should be taught, in what order, and at what age. In recent years, politicians and bureaucrats have further dictated when and how this content will be tested, how schools will be graded, and how teachers will be evaluated. We are in the strong arms of a top-down Taylorian approach to every aspect of managing public education.

Changing Old Habits

Changing the habits of adults is a challenge. Often we are barely conscious of our routines; these are just the patterns of our days. While many adult patterns of behavior will be different in a quality competency based learning environment, in this section we will highlight three patterns that are ripe for change.

A competency based learning model challenges many of the standard practices of this authoritarian style. The competency based learning model assumes that teachers understand their students well enough to adjust the instructional plan, assumes that teachers work with students to determine learning interests and styles, and assumes that teachers work together to help each other grow expert in observational and systematic assessment as well as differentiated instruction to meet student learning needs. Teachers who are comfortable following a top-down instructional and assessment plan will have many new habits and skills to learn.

Educators will also be challenged to learn to **balance coverage with competency** in a school that embraces competency based learning. A comprehensive plan for instruction will embrace exploration and enrichment, which might well include whole class learning and a curriculum plan for covering content at a grade or stage in student development. But competency in essential skills will be a priority over keeping up with an overwhelming pacing guide.

Learning for enrichment, exploration, and pure pleasure are crucial for a well-rounded education. In the CBL world, we will look for ways to embrace pathways to competency, along with many opportunities to stretch awareness, stimulate curiosity, and develop enthusiastic learners for life. Teacher leaders, administrative leaders, and parents working together are challenged to create new models of instruction that will establish pathways to competency within a culture of scholarship.

As we move toward competency based learning systems, we will need **clear exit standards** for graduation from high school, course completion, and certificate or university degree completion. There may be differences between the desired exit outcomes of communities based on culture, geography, or the needs of local employers. There may be differences among the exit outcomes developed by different institutions based on the expertise and interests of community leaders. Students and their families will face choices between institutions that have different visions for student learning.

We will need clear **standards for competency at every step along the pathway** to our long-term learning outcomes. Once exit outcomes are established, it will be our responsibility to establish a framework of competencies that allows students to fully develop the skills and knowledge that leads to the exit outcomes.

If you are an educator during the advent of competency based learning, opportunities for learning and collaboration await. For most schools and districts, creating the conditions for safe and collaborative adult learning and identifying key learning skills or outcomes for all staff will be among the first steps toward competency based learning.

17

Learning for Understanding and Application

I remember learning to sail on Lake Charlevoix in northern Michigan. For years, I'd watched the beautiful boats tighten their sails and lean into the wind, come about and elegantly shift direction, or fly downwind with mainsail and spinnaker out wide and full. In my small sailboat, I practiced tightening my sails and heading as close into the wind as possible, changing tack and moving across the direction of the wind, shifting the rudder and releasing the sail at just the right moment so that I could catch the wind and gracefully find my new tack.

Often, at first, it was not so graceful. When changing direction, the boom might crack my head when I forgot to duck at the right moment. Sometimes my timing was poor, and I failed to build up enough speed to complete the change of direction, and my sails would flap helplessly as the wind tossed me about. But, occasionally, I would get it right.

"Coming about," I'd yell, even if I was all alone in the small boat. Build up the speed, shift the rudder hard, release the sail, duck, hold the rudder, catch the sail on the other side of the mast, and bind the line. Then the wind would fill the sails and the mast would arch, and the boat would catch its speed and shoot forward in a new direction. I'd sail for hours, loving every turn, every long run into the wind, every failure, and every moment of grace.

Learning is joyful. As humans, with our oversized cerebral and prefrontal cortex, we are wired to learn. When we have learning goals that are clear, attainable, and personally meaningful, a gang of thugs could not deter our desire to learn.

Competency based learning is focused on student learning outcomes and is built with the following design principles in mind:

♦ Students advance upon mastery, not age;
♦ The pathway to competency is built with explicit and measurable learning objectives;
♦ Assessment is primarily formative, and skills or concepts are assessed in multiple contexts to guarantee both deep understanding and application.

A child watches in wonder as her parent reads a story. Her mom can decipher the squiggly symbols on a page, use her voice to convey excitement or danger, sadness or love, and make characters come alive. At some point, the child learns that this magic we call reading can be hers. Step by step, adults help her learn to read. "What's this word?" "Now try to read the whole sentence." At every step, the goals are clear. At every step, the goals are attainable. This child believes she can learn to read. She wants to read, and she wants to practice reading.

In a musical family, a child is given a guitar. For years, other members of the family have made instruments come alive, and now it's his turn, his instrument, his desire. Every new chord is a victory. Every new song is a celebration. Every day he finds time to practice. Every day he is a step closer to his goal.

An adolescent is focused on her video game. The graphics are great, and the content intriguing. She is at level three and so close to level four. If she could only kill a few more gorgons or remember to get help from the lady with the light saber who is hiding in the second cave after the river crossing. For hours, she sits absorbed in her game. She never meant to spend all day indoors, but she is so close to getting to the next level.

In her kindergarten class, a student is learning to subitize, quickly recognize the number value of a group. Not all of the kids can do it. In the math center, she works in a small group with her teacher, who shows her one side of the domino and points to a group of dots. "Six," she correctly identifies. They play with dice and dominoes for a few minutes, and the students almost always gets the answer quickly, without having to slow down and count each dot. The next day, the teacher brings out an abacus at the math center and moves a group of beads on the top row. "How many?" she asks, and every time a student gets it right there are smiles. The next day, the teacher has paper plates on which she has drawn sets of objects from two to ten. Every day it is something new. She learns to recognize the value of a group of buttons, beads, or checkers, or a value on the abacus, or a group of bean bags on the floor, or the number of chairs at a large table. Every day she looks forward to going to the math center. The teacher has a wonderful way of making it challenging but never so hard that it seems impossible.

On weekends, a third grade student watches baseball with his dad. It is a special time. They cheer, they root for their team, and, after the game, they go outside and play catch. This child dreams of being a ball player. During the week, he keeps a ball and glove in his backpack, just in case there might be someone who wants to play catch. At home during the week, he practices throwing the ball on the garage roof and catching it as it comes flying over the gutters. He's learned to catch almost anything that is thrown his way, on the ground or in the air. He can't wait for the spring baseball leagues to begin.

Read Chapter 9 and answer the multiple choice questions at the end. The learning goals of this assignment are entirely unclear. For some students, the content of the chapter or the reading level may be too difficult, and this makes learning success unattainable. For other students, the content may already be familiar, and nothing new is learned. In almost all cases, this kind of assignment is not personally meaningful and is presented as

FIGURE 17.1 Factors Influencing Intrinsic Motivation

something you must do and for which you will be punished with lousy grades if you answer the questions poorly.

Finish this Word Search worksheet before the end of the class, and if you don't get it done, take it as homework. If there are any imaginable learning goals for this assignment, they are unclear to most of us. For some, this activity is drudgery, but possible. For others, the activity is both difficult and drudgery. Only creatures from the Talarian Republic find this activity personally meaningful.

There are two weeks left in the semester and three more chapters to cover. Get ready, here it comes. Whenever teaching and learning becomes a race, deep understanding suffers. Whenever the learning goals are to memorize a bunch of content to pass a test, the essence of learning has been perverted. After years of extrinsic direction to learn content that has little personal meaning, often boring, occasionally impossible, many students experience a diminution of intrinsic motivation to learn (Figure 17.1). Young children are naturally drawn to learning in every aspect of life, but after enough years of CTS, this love of learning can be lost.

Consider the possibilities that come from a well-designed competency based learning system to help more children develop the skills and habits that allow them to love learning for life.

Clear Learning Goals

When students have a clear goal for learning, they are more able to stay focused on giving effort to achieve this outcome. *I want to be a good reader like Mom. I want to be able to quickly recognize the number groups. I want to catch every ball Dad throws to me.*

Finish the chapter is not a learning goal. *Try to do better* is not a clear goal. *Get a better grade* is a compliance goal. *Bring treats to class for extra credit* has nothing to do with authentic learning outcomes. When students can clearly understand and visualize learning goals, they become real. They become attainable. It is possible to contrast the skills you have today with the outcomes you want and be motivated to engage in a learning plan that helps you reach your goal.

Competency based learning pathways will have long-term goals (skills, knowledge, units, graduation, certification, or employment eligibility) with clear step-by-step increments of learning and skill that lead to these goals. Some students may wish to travel farther down a particular learning pathway than others, but every student will know where she is and where she wants to be in every crucial aspect of development.

Attainable Learning Goals

When students believe that an outcome is possible for them, within their grasp, available to them with reasonable effort, they try harder. All the research on instructional match, instructional zone, and zone of proximal development makes it clear that students are more motivated, spend more time on task, and behave better when the learning task is just a bit challenging without pushing them into the frustration zone (Burns, 2007; Fuchs & Fuchs, 1988; Gickling & Armstrong, 1978; Vygotsky, 1978; Betts, 1946).

Time in the frustration zone pushes kids into disengagement. Patterns of disengagement can impact children for the rest of their lives. When a child with a third grade reading level is given reading material at the fifth grade level, frustration is not far away. Rigid learning programs put many students at risk for the simple reason that they are not all at the same level of readiness.

The importance of allowing students to learn at the appropriate instructional level is one of the most well-established points in all the literature on teaching and learning. Yet curriculum-driven instruction trumps instructional match in CTS classrooms and schools across the nation and around the world.

Every time a student says (or thinks), "I'm not good at math," it is likely an expression of poor learning experiences based on a curriculum-driven learning model. A few months or a few years of working unsuccessfully to keep up with the pace of instruction is enough for most kids to give up on a subject matter or, in some cases, to give up on themselves.

Often, there are some other students in class who lack motivation to learn for a very different reason. They are bored. They already know the skill or subject matter and going through the lessons and practice sheets is an exercise in compliance to an uncaring authority. For these students, the learning goals are not "attainable" because they have already been attained. Gaming designers understand this and create higher levels of challenge within the structure of their product. Rigidly paced learning programs in school have not yet responded to this obvious need.

In a competency based learning system, the steps along the pathway are clearly delineated. Once competency is attained for a crucial skill, educators look for ways to move the student on to the next skill along the pathway.

Personally Meaningful Goals

Making learning goals clear and attainable significantly increases motivation and its byproducts, including time on task, attention, and rates of learning. But when you help students understand why a learning goal is important in their personal lives, and when you offer some opportunity to choose the skills or content that will be included in their learning program, motivation soars (Ames, 1992; Csikszentmihalyi, 1985; Driscoll, 1994; Lepper & Hoddell, 1989; Mayer, 2002; Stiggins, 1999).

With young children, it is often as simple as letting them pick an activity center or a book. As students get older, allowing them to participate in the planning of their learning process makes it more likely that you will see great effort and outcomes. Projects and activities that support progress along a competency pathway can easily be personalized. By middle and high school, students are capable of making choices regarding which content and/or skills they want to develop to a proficient level, and for which content/skills they would like to excel and go beyond typical standards for competency. Post high school learning should certainly include student planning input, with the end goal of competency within a personally designed learning plan.

> We can never attain first-rate learning outcomes with a ram-it-down-their-throats approach to teaching students. Competency based learning gives us an opportunity to create a system that offers clear, attainable, and personally meaningful learning goals. By nurturing the intrinsic desire to learn and the joy of learning, we can help more of our students become successful learners for life.

For students to take ownership of their own learning, observant parents and teachers watch carefully to see what special interest a child demonstrates. They allow time for exploration, play, and discovery before dumping too much content over the intrinsic fires of learning. Sometimes great teachers step back, watch and listen, perceive the direction in which student interest is developing, and only then provide challenges and opportunities to further excite the desire to learn.

Learning systems that give students a chance to move from competency to competency will enhance intrinsic motivation. They will help students see the connection between effort and the rewards of learning. And they could create generations of learners who understand that meaningful learning is possible any time, any place, and at any pace.

18

Masters of the Trade
Game Designers

The designers of video games have applied the principles of competency based learning, in combination with other fundamental learning concepts, arguably better than anyone. You might question the content that some game creators use or the purposefulness of the activities, but you cannot question the efficacy of their design principles to interest gamers, hold attention, make it fun, and motivate players to want to come back for more. Consider these learning concepts and principles, which are clearly demonstrated in high quality digital games.

Students Advance upon Mastery, Not Age

Games have levels of challenge and start with the acquisition of basic skills that are needed for success throughout the game. Models of success, video examples, or prompts are used to help gamers find success at the earliest levels. Players are never pushed to a higher level based on age, time given to the task, or any other reason until they are capable of success at the next level.

Tiered Learning

Vygotsky would be proud of the care with which designers craft tiers of learning. With every new level, the knowledge and skills picked up in previous levels can be applied to help the gamer be successful. Sometimes a skill or idea is introduced at one level, and then opportunities to use or practice that skill become available after several more steps have been mastered. At lower levels, players are taught to use skills within a simple context. As they progress through the levels, the skill is used within a more complex situation or used in combination with other skills.

Instructional Zone

Success breeds success, unless it comes too easily. Designers artfully apply the research on instructional match, instructional zone, and zone of proximal development. The player is challenged enough so that she never gets bored. She is highly engaged and motivated by the challenge. The player is also never challenged to the point that she disengages and wants to quit. Designers write exquisite algorithms to balance the need for a high degree of success and just enough challenge.

Trial and Error

The games encourage players to try something, see if it works, reflect, form a hypothesis, visualize an action plan, try something new, and repeat the process. Within a carefully designed plan for each player to be successful, reaching your goals can only occur through action. Players learn to try stuff and see what works. This feedback loop is quick and consistent.

Explicit Learning Objectives

The pathway to success is built with explicit objectives. Players know what they are trying to achieve. They are glad to give effort to achieve this clear objective and are happy to learn from the experiences of others. With explicit goals, gamers become problem-solvers, using previously acquired knowledge along with skills and tactics.

Motivation to Take On Challenges

Successful video games are difficult. Gamers want to take on challenges, solve problems, collaborate, and persist. Gamers intrinsically want to learn more skills and get better at the game. Contrast that with students in many classrooms who want to do as little as possible to get a good grade, as judged by someone else, when working on obscure and personally meaningless learning objectives.

Embedded Assessment

Game designers do not use end of unit assessments, and they don't give grades. There is no bell curve. Instead, assessment is embedded into every moment of the game. The level of difficulty is increased only when the student is ready for the challenge, as demonstrated by her level of play. Every moment of play is used as part of the formative assessment process to determine whether to present new challenges or take the player to the next level.

Identity and Networks of Support

Gamers see themselves as learning and getting better, with the end goal of beating the game or an opponent. They often form support networks with friends or colleagues who share tactics, experiences, and suggestions for improvement. With every new skill, with every new level, with every victory, their identity as a learner is reinforced.

Competency based learning systems have the potential to take learning to a whole new level for our society. When combined with good learning principles, and a little common sense, we can design learning systems at school, at home, and in our communities that bring learning to life for generations of children and adults. While video game designers want to sell games and keep gamers engaged, they nonetheless have applied the research on motivation and learning far better than most school district instructional leaders.

19

State Competency Based Learning Initiatives

A large majority of states have some provision in state regulations that allows school districts to opt out of traditional Carnegie unit seat time requirements for graduation.

Alabama policy states that "one credit may be granted in Grade 9–12 for required or elective course consisting of a minimum of 140 instructional hours **or** in which students demonstrate mastery of Alabama course of study content standards in one-credit courses without specified instructional time." Kentucky allows schools to award competency based credits if they have developed specific criteria for determining proficiency. Oregon was among the first states to enable districts to develop proficiency systems for the awarding of credit and has supported the development of competency based learning pilot sites. Iowa allows both competency based and time-based credits for graduation. Ohio allows credit flexibility based on a state approved waiver system and permits districts to include distance learning, after school programming, internships, and community service as part of their pathways to competency.

Since 2005, New Hampshire has taken a leadership position in the development of competency based learning systems. The state legislature approved new *Minimum Standards for Public School Approval*, under which districts were required to create standards for competency and begin measuring course credit in these terms by the start of the 2009–10 school year. This was the first statewide effort to create a competency based learning system, and the minimum standards have been subsequently updated (New Hampshire DOE, 2014).

Local districts were given broad discretion in the interpretation and implementation of the New Hampshire competency mandate. Some districts became quickly invested in the opportunity to build flexible, personalized programming, while others have stayed with more familiar curriculum-driven methodologies. But state leadership in New Hampshire has persisted toward a different learning model. A guide for districts, *New Hampshire's Vision for Redesign, Moving from High Schools to Learning Communities*, was approved (New Hampshire DOE, 2007). New teacher training regulations were approved in 2011, and administrative rules were updated in 2014 to further support the transition toward competency based learning. A collection of resources developed by New Hampshire educators to support extended learning opportunities are available at beyondclassroom.org.

One of the factors motivating change in New Hampshire is the desire to reduce the incidence of high school dropouts. In addition to the state mandate to create more personalized competency based learning options, the age at which a student could drop out of school was raised to 18. In 2002, 25 percent of high school students dropped out before graduation. By 2011, the rate was 4.68 percent and falling.

Maine has developed a strategic plan for learner centered instruction, *Education Evolving: Maine's Plan for Putting Learners First* (Maine DOE, 2012). The core priorities of the plan include:

- ◆ Effective, Learner-Centered Instruction;
- ◆ Great Teachers and Leaders;
- ◆ Multiple Pathways for Learner Achievement;
- ◆ Comprehensive School and Community Supports;
- ◆ Coordinated and Effective State Support.

Beginning in 2015, students in Maine must demonstrate proficiency in English, math, science, social studies, and health/

physical education for graduation. By 2018, additional competency requirements will be in place.

Vermont requires districts to establish standards of proficiency for graduation, to use tiered systems of support to assist all students working toward the standards, and to develop personalized learning plans for students in Grades 7–12. This state's Education Quality Standards provides a clear definition of CBL but uses the word "proficiency" in its wording.

> "Proficiency-based learning" and "proficiency-based graduation" refers to systems of instruction, assessment, grading, and academic reporting that are based on students demonstrating mastery of the knowledge and skills they are expected to learn before they progress to the next lesson, get promoted to the next grade level, or receive a diploma.
> —Vermont Education Quality Standards (State of Vermont Board of Education, 2013)

Colorado has approved a multi-year process of developing and implementing state guidelines for graduation requirements. Starting with ninth graders in 2017–18, and with full implementation by 2020–21, these guidelines will include new academic standards and individual career and academic plans for each student. Local school districts will be able to select options by which their students can demonstrate competency, with options to include coursework, minimum scores on state or national tests, rigorous learning projects, college level courses, and professional certificates. Colorado predicts that by 2020, 74 percent of jobs in Colorado will require education beyond high school (Colorado Dept. of Education, 2013).

The Council of Chief State School Officers (CCSSO) has developed the Innovation Lab Network (ILN) to share learning, drive collective action, and to create and scale student-centered learning environments. In their publication, *Innovation in Action: State*

Pathways for Advancing Student Centered Learning (CCSSO, 2015), they call for states to:

- ◆ Define and systematize college and career readiness consistent with deeper learning;
- ◆ Enable personalized learning and prepare the educator workforce so that all students can succeed;
- ◆ Establish balanced systems of assessment to meaningfully measure college and career readiness;
- ◆ Anchor accountability in college and career readiness;
- ◆ Develop seamless pathways to college and career.

The development and use of competency based learning, while not a new idea, presents many opportunities for innovation. States can serve as incubators for that innovation, and hopefully we can all reap the bounty of the best ideas that are emerging in every corner of the nation.

Innovation is the creation and development of new ideas.

- ◆ Which states will abandon the Carnegie unit and course credit requirement system for high school altogether and replace it with a clearly defined set of outcome competencies?
- ◆ Will some states move to a competency certificate program, specifically describing the knowledge and skills students have developed to proficiency?
- ◆ Might states choose differing sets of outcomes as crucial to life readiness based on their assessment of the needs of their citizens and workforce in the future?
- ◆ Who will develop explicit pathways to their college and career readiness standards and use technology systems to help track individual progress?
- ◆ Which states will recognize the importance of competency based learning systems and develop statewide systems to help more children build crucial foundation skills during the early childhood years?

20

Competency Based Learning in Post-Secondary Education

Post-secondary education has responded more vigorously to the opportunities presented by competency based learning than any other segment of the education system. Colleges, universities, community colleges, technical schools, and certification programs compete for students and are becoming responsive to the needs of adult learners who come to higher education knowing different things, needing different outcomes, and learning at different rates and in different ways.

These schools/organizations are also responding to poor program completion rates and the concern that many college degrees are irrelevant to the needs of the workplace. They are finding ways to use the availability of technology for instruction, assessment, and personalization of learning. While medical and vocational/technical training programs have long included a competency based component, the application of competency to other degree and certificate programs is quickly developing.

In the 1970s, competency based learning programs at institutes for higher learning began to emerge, in part because of a concern for the growing number of adults returning to college. Colleges began to develop prior learning assessments (PLA) to acknowledge learning from other institutions, from military training, or other sources. Generally these competencies were then translated into course-based college credits. Innovative college programs emerged at Empire State College, Regents College, Thomas Edison State College, Alverno College, DePaul University's School for New Learning, and other institutions.

With the advent of online learning, Institutions of Higher Education (IHEs) began to grapple with the uncomfortable problem of assigning credit for learning that did not take place in the classroom and, therefore, could not be measured in class hours per week. No one could know exactly how much time an online student spent on a learning module or test. As measurement of time became less reliable, measurement of learning became more important.

Measurement of learning continues to increase in importance. The need for more adults to access relevant skill-based post-secondary training, the availability of free Massive Open Online Courses (MOOCs), the quality and availability of digital learning programs, and the desire for more personalized learning programs have made universities and other learning institutions increasingly offer competency based learning options for their students.

Every month it seems more options become available. Some institutions use competency frameworks within a course-based system. This approach may include testing out, assignment of credit for previous life experiences, blended learning, and/or the completion of online modules to earn course credit. This maintains the familiar credit structure found in most colleges and universities.

Other institutions have stepped away from the credit/course model. They start by establishing clear competency exit outcomes for a degree or certificate and assessing the student's level of knowledge and skill in relation to these outcomes. Additional learning goals based on student interest are considered. A learning program is designed to match the needs of each student, which could include courses, MOOCs, internships, projects, independent study, or other experiences. A coach or mentor works with the student to facilitate learning and assess progress. Cohort groups may be used to further support learning. And only when the student has demonstrated competency in each essential program outcome is the degree or certificate awarded.

Western Governors University was chartered in 1996, supported by the Western Governors Association, to use competencies rather than seat time as the measure of its outcomes and to take advantage of distance learning opportunities. It has grown to become an accredited national university, with more than 50,000 students in all fifty states, offering competency-based degrees at the associate, bachelor, and master's levels. WGU's online programs use tests, projects, papers, and practical demonstrations of a required skill to demonstrate mastery and allow students to advance upon competency rather than using time-limited course options. At WGU, there are no required courses, just required competencies. Working with a faculty advisor, students work out a personalized plan for reaching the competencies required in a program and are charged a flat fee per term rather than by credit hours.

At DePaul University's School for New Learning (SNL), students earn degrees by demonstrating the competencies required for the degree. They can take courses that are related to those competencies or develop portfolios that demonstrate mastery of those competencies through prior learning. Some coursework is required.

Excelsior College School of Nursing has offered an accredited competency based associates degree for almost four decades. The program is designed for students transitioning from a Licensed Practical Nurse to a Registered Nurse role or coming to nursing with a clinical background. Students complete general education requirements through coursework, must successfully demonstrate nursing clinical skills, and must pass a computer simulation examination measuring clinical competence.

The University of Maine at Presque Isle has begun a multi-year process to base all of its academic programs on "proficiencies" that students must master to earn a degree. Students will progress through in-person, online, and hybrid degree programs by demonstrating proficiency in required concepts. Northern Arizona University students pay a flat $2,500 for a six-month "subscription" to classes at NAU. During that time, they are free to take—and earn credit for—as many online courses as possible within three available undergraduate degree programs. Capella

University has mapped academic and professional standards to all degree programs, and its FlexPath allows students to complete as many courses per quarter as they can for one flat tuition rate in the departments of business, information technology, and psychology. Davenport University offers an online self-paced competency based MBA.

Even large public universities have made the move toward competency based learning. The University of Wisconsin offers its Flexible Option, comprised of five competency-based online programs leading to a certificate or bachelor's degree. Purdue University offers a transdisciplinary bachelor's degree program based on learned and demonstrated competencies at the Purdue Polytechnic Institute and the College of Technology.

The University of Michigan has approved a master's degree program for health profession educators, partly in response to a national shortage of medical school faculty. The MHPE program prepares practicing professionals in medicine, nursing, dentistry, pharmacy, public health, social work and other health professions to become health profession educators. This competency based degree is not based on credit hour requirements.

MPHE students choose from among 21 competencies that are tied to various health professions. Each enrolling student's experience and previous learning is reviewed by a competency assessment panel and then assigned credit for existing competencies. Students are assigned a mentor, and an individualize program is designed to meet the needs of each student. The pace of the program is flexible. For the degree, students must provide documentation and evidence of competency, which could be a paper, video presentation, PowerPoint, grant application, portfolio, or some combination of multiple pieces of evidence, and pass a final summative assessment based on their learning portfolio.

Interest in higher education CBE continues to pick up steam. In July 2014, the US House passed H.R. 3136, the Advancing Competency-Based Education Demonstration Project Act. The vote was unanimous, 414–0.

Competency based learning has emerged as a viable model for post-secondary education. But as each new CBE program is developed, there are questions. How do we define specific required competencies? Are some competencies more important than others? Can there be different levels of competency? Can a student add personally meaningful competencies to a degree or certificate plan? Are there multiple pathways to a given competency? What are the acceptable demonstrations of competency? Do our proofs/demonstrations accurately describe the ability to understand a body of knowledge, develop a skill, or apply this skill? How do we train faculty to use consistent and effective assessment protocols? How do we train faculty to be skilled at differentiation of the learning experience? What is the role of credit or grades, and how can these be transferred from one institution to another? As competency based learning blends with and, in some cases replaces, curriculum-driven methodologies, how do we ensure quality?

> The issue of quality among competency based learning systems is pressing. Some institutions of higher education, in the race to find more students or sell more credits, might choose a less demanding road to CBE. For those institutions considering a move to competency based learning, consider this rubric for quality CBE.

A Rubric for Considering the Quality of IHE Competency Based Learning Initiatives

Level 1

- ◆ A set of knowledge competencies has been established for each course;
- ◆ Students work to achieve these competencies by the end of semester/year;
- ◆ Students who do not achieve every competency will repeat the course.

Level 2

- A set of knowledge competencies has been established for each course;
- Students can test out of courses in which they have expertise and experience;
- Students can move through course modules or chapters at their own pace;
- Passing chapter/module tests and completion of other required assignments (papers, journals, etc.) is considered completion of course credit and/or competency;
- Community service, internships, observation, performance groups, or similar experiences will be considered as the equivalent to a required course or competency.

Level 3

- Competencies for each required course are clearly established, including knowledge, skill, and application;
- Students are assessed to determine existing knowledge/skill/application levels and can test out of a course by demonstrating knowledge, skill, and application;
- Students have personalized learning plans focused on achieving the required learning objectives at their own pace;
- Learning plans can include specific modules, learning materials, or experiences;
- Students receive frequent and systematic assessment of progress;
- Timely support is available;
- Students advance upon demonstrated mastery of learning goals leading to required competencies.

Level 4

- Minimum competencies are established for a certificate or degree, including knowledge, skill, and application;

- A review/assessment of knowledge, skill, and application helps determine each student's learning needs within the program;
- Personalized learning plans focus on achievement of the required competencies;
- Specific short term learning plans are developed by the facilitator and student and can include specific modules, learning materials, or experiences;
- Students receive frequent and systematic assessment of progress;
- Timely support is available;
- Students advance upon demonstrated mastery of learning goals leading to required competencies;
- Degree or certificate is awarded upon demonstration of all required competencies.

Level 5

- Minimum competencies are established for a certificate or degree, including knowledge, skill, and application;
- Additional learning goals are established based on the individual needs and interests of the student;
- A review/assessment of knowledge, skill, and application helps determine each student's learning needs within the program;
- A review/assessment of the student's learning strengths and style helps contribute to the development of a personalized learning plan;
- Personalized learning plans focus on achievement of the required competencies and the student's chosen goals;
- Specific short term learning plans are developed by the facilitator and student and can include specific modules, learning materials, or experiences;
- Cohort groups, online networks, or other support group structures are available;
- Students receive frequent and systematic assessment of progress;

- Timely instructional support is available;
- Students advance upon demonstrated mastery of learning goals leading to required competencies and student-initiated learning goals;
- Degree or certificate is awarded upon demonstration of all required competencies.

As competency based learning continues to expand within post-secondary education, professional organizations are stepping up to provide leadership and establish standards of practice. The American Association of Colleges and Universities (AAC&U) developed the Liberal Education and America's Promise (LEAP) initiative, which champions the importance of a 21st century liberal education. LEAP has identified "Essential Learning Outcomes," covering broad knowledge areas, cognitive and practical skills, and the application of knowledge and skill to complex problems.

The Lumina Foundation developed the Degree Qualifications Profile (DQP) to provide a baseline set of reference points for what students should know and be able to do to earn an associate's, bachelor's, and master's degree. The DQP defines educational outcomes in terms of what graduates know and can do in the areas of applied learning, intellectual skills, specialized knowledge, broad knowledge, and civic learning.

The Western Association of Schools and Colleges, the Higher Learning Commission, the Southern Association of Colleges and Schools, the Council of Independent Colleges and Universities, and several universities are working with the Lumina Foundation to test and further develop the DQP.

The Association of American Colleges and Universities is developing a competency based framework for undergraduate education called General Education Maps and Markers (GEMs) to align with the Degree Qualifications Profile (DQP).

The Global Learning Qualifications Profile (GLQP) was developed by Open SUNY, based in part on the LEAP project's essential learning outcomes and rubrics. The GLQP emphasizes assessment of college-level outcomes obtained through open learning sources, including Open Educational Resources (OERs),

Massive Open Online Courses (MOOCs), and prior or experiential learning.

The National Association of Manufacturers' Manufacturing Skills Certification System has developed a structure of stackable credentials indicating that workers have attained competencies for increasingly sophisticated levels of work across many areas of manufacturing, from machine operator to engineer to management positions. The essential elements of the Skills Certification System are:

♦ A collection of competencies that together defines a successful, high-performance manufacturing workforce;
♦ Industry-driven certifications that align with competencies;
♦ Best-in-class curriculum to articulate into for-credit education pathways that will ensure students achieve the competencies necessary to achieve industry credentials.

> Post-secondary education has discovered competency based learning, and the process of experimentation and innovation has begun.

The limitations of a time-bound learning system are starting to be widely recognized among the public and institutions of higher learning (Laitinen, 2012). When many university graduates cannot find professional jobs, and when growing businesses can't find new employees with the skills needed for success on the job, a new model begins to emerge. There are tens of millions of adults of all ages who need to complete a degree, earn a certificate, or update skills to match the changing job requirements of the information and technology society, for whom a competency based learning system just makes sense.

As we step free of the time-bound system, we must create a competency based system that truly measures learning, that is clear in describing its learning objectives and transparent in its practice of measuring progress toward competency. Higher education is asked to do so many things, from offering training for specific technical skills to nurturing poets and artists, from developing well-rounded leaders to training scientists and researchers with eclectic interests and specific knowledge and skills. As the need for better, faster, and more flexible pathways to modern job skills continues to push us toward competency based learning, we are challenged to find the balance between liberal education, civic and character education, and technical learning. We are at the dawn of the age of personalized, flexible, lifelong learning.

21

Competency Based Learning in Secondary Schools

Much of the attention given to competency based learning has been at the secondary level and focused on reaching standards for high school graduation. The conventional pattern of required classes and credits for high school graduation presents a litany of obvious questions. Why can't participation in sports take the place of a required PE credit? Can a student who takes advanced math from Kumon or Khan be given credit? Why do we push some kids through the curriculum when we know they are not ready? Why do we require that other kids take classes in which they are already proficient? Do all students learn best with 180 days of instruction? Why exactly do we take summers off?

In recent years, many of the questions have been related to economic and social concerns. Does graduation from high school mean anything? Are graduates ready for employment? Are they ready for college? Does a diploma indicate that basic math and reading skills are in place? Are graduating students prepared to be lifelong learners? What does graduation mean? Does our system stack the deck against poor children?

Nations around the world have recognized the need to improve education outcomes in response to new social, economic, and technical realities. The European Union has identified key competencies in its *Key Competences for Lifelong Learning: European Reference Framework* (European Commission, 2007). This framework defines eight key competences and describes the essential knowledge, skills, and attitudes related to each of these. These key competences are: communication in the mother tongue, communication in foreign languages, math competence, and basic competence in science and technology, digital competence, learning to learn, social and civic competencies, sense of initiative and entrepreneurship, and cultural awareness and expression. Each of the 28 European Union nations is approaching competency based learning in its own way.

Finland's approach includes a systemic approach to individualization of learning in the tenth through twelfth grades. Students build their personalized learning schedule made up of 70 minute classes, six week units, and the opportunity to progress at their own pace.

In Sweden, a group of 33 Kunskapsskolan (knowledge schools) operates with personalized learning pathways in which students track their own learning progress, beginning in eighth grade. Three levels of student mastery of competencies along the learning pathways is available, to be chosen with the advice of a personal coach.

In British Columbia, a strong initiative supporting personalized learning and the development of competency is described in the *British Columbia Education Plan* (British Columbia Ministry of Eduction, 2015) and detailed in *Exploring Curriculum Design, Transforming Curriculum and Assessment* (British Columbia Ministry of Eduction, 2013). Alberta's development plan for competency based learning is described in *Framework for Student Learning: Competencies for Engaged Thinkers and Ethical Citizens with an Entrepreneurial Spirit* (Alberta Education, 2011).

Competency based learning is the recognized training method for vocational education and training (VET) in Australia. National standards define general competencies in the workplace, and specific units of competency can be set for an industry or a specific enterprise. In most Australian states, students can access this training at age 16, with more than half of all VET students over the age of 25.

In the United States, with permissive language allowing competency based alternatives to Carnegie units based on seat time available in most states, new models of competency based learning are emerging. Changing from a curriculum-driven to a competency based model is challenging, much like redesigning an airplane while it's still flying through the air. But a small group of leaders in local school districts and schools across the nation have stepped up to the task.

In New Hampshire, with its strong state-level competency initiative, districts have embraced competency to different degrees. In some schools, required high school classes are aligned with competencies and graduation is based on competency, but students are not yet able to move at a flexible or individualized pace. Some schools have used technology or digital learning to complement traditional classroom instruction. Other schools have more vigorously pursued options including testing out, extended learning opportunities outside of the traditional class-room (apprenticeships, community service, independent study, internships, performing groups, private instruction), project based learning, authentic assessment, portfolios, and blended and/or digital learning.

New Hampshire Schools Are Adopting Competency Based Learning in Varied Ways

Almost a quarter of the 250+ students at Pittsfield Middle-High School spend part of the school day, after-school hours, or summertime earning credits through activities outside regular classes, such as assisting dentists, accompanying midwives, designing websites, volunteering in kindergarten classrooms, or working at local newspapers. They earn both core and elective credits for such activities, produce a portfolio of work, and offer presentations to show they've developed competencies.

Teachers at Newfound Regional High School in Bristol, NH, have worked to develop competencies that allow for more interdisciplinary work and thematic projects. Rather than using prescribed performance tasks for each competency, the NRHS model emphasizes that mastery can be shown in different ways, and students are given some choice in how they will demonstrate competency.

Virtual Learning Academy Charter School was the first NH statewide online school. Their courses are aligned to the NH state competencies. Students must show at least 85 percent proficiency in each course competency to pass a course. Targeted lessons help students master any specific competencies with which they are struggling.

North Country Charter Academy is an alternative high school that serves dropouts or students at-risk of dropping out. Most of the school curriculum is delivered using an online course provider. Students attend school sites at which they use the digital learning program and move at a flexible pace with additional face-to-face support from teachers.

Sanborn Regional High School uses a competency based model in which students are given supports on an ongoing basis, with time set aside each day for catch up or acceleration of progress. Students who score below a certain level have the option to retake an exam to achieve mastery. Sanborn was one of the earliest schools in NH to adopt a competency based learning model.

Lindsay Unified School District is a high-poverty and high-ELL district in California. In response to many years of low achievement, LUSD defined the knowledge and skills required of Lindsay students in all content areas and developed units of study for each learning standard in consultation with the Marzano Research Laboratory, Reinventing Schools Coalition, Rural Education for Americans Project, and Schwahn Leadership Associates. Beginning in 2009, the performance-based system was applied at the ninth grade, expanded to seventh to tenth grades in 2010, and then rolled out to include K-12. The LUSD design aims to meet learners at their level of instruction, allows learners to go back or move forward in any topic, and adopts an any-place any-time approach to learning. In 2012, LUSD won a $10 million Race to the Top grant.

Competency based learning is an essential part of high school to career programming. The Advanced Technology Academy and the Advanced Photonic Academy, in Albuquerque, New Mexico, are examples. These academies are the focus of a collaboration between Sandia National Laboratories, Central New Mexico Community College, and the University of New Mexico.

The Alamo Area Aerospace Academy (AAAA) is a collaboration of businesses and schools in San Antonio, and students spend half the day in high school and the other half learning aerospace maintenance, airframe and power plant mechanics, and other skill sets which may lead to employment or to continued education. In San Antonio, approximately 16 percent of Lockheed Martin's workforce is hired directly from the AAAA.

Penn Medicine teamed up with schools in the Philadelphia area to create the Penn Medicine High School Pipeline Program. This program enables students from lower socio-economic programs to choose among nursing, allied health care, or nonclinical healthcare tracks like finance or patient services, and offers incentives for students to enroll in continuing education after high school.

The Academy for Technology Excellence in Ft. Myers, Florida, was started as a collaboration between Dunbar High School and local businesses, including Microsoft, Chico's, First Community Bank, and other employers. Serving mostly students from poor households since 2005, the program trains students in 18 computer certifications and other skill areas, offers paid internships, and up to 48 postsecondary credits. Employers need skilled employees, and competency delivers rewarding jobs.

Chugach School District serves more than 200 students over a 20,000 square mile portion of south central Alaska. More than 70 percent of students are home-schoolers. In response to poor outcomes, in 1994 the district began a transition to competency based learning. Within five years, average student achievement on the California Achievement Test rose from the bottom quartile to the 72nd percentile. By 2000, student participation in college entrance exams rose from zero to more than 70 percent. In 2001, CSD was given the prestigious Malcolm Baldrige National Quality Award and in 2009 was selected as a recipient of the APEX Excellence Award. The story of Chugach is well told in *Delivering on the Promise* (2008), by Richard DeLorenzo, Wendy Battino, Rick Schreiber, and Barbara Gaddy-Carrio.

The CSD curriculum is based upon a continuum of standards in the ten content areas identified as essential. These essential content areas include mathematics, technology, social science, reading, writing, cultural awareness, personal/social/health, career development, service learning, and science. Each student has an individual learning plan and advances through the key elements of each continuum at their own individual pace, aiming to meet or exceed the graduation level in each content area.

As yet there is no consensus regarding the key elements needed for a competency based high school graduation. New Hampshire has its defined competencies for graduation. The SCANS recommendations include five broadly defined competencies and three areas of foundation skill. The Hewlett Foundation's Deeper Learning framework identifies six inter-connected competencies essential for 21st century college and career readiness, including mastering core academic content, thinking critically and solving complex problems, working collaboratively, communicating effectively, learning how to learn, and developing academic mindsets. The EU identifies its *European Framework of Key Competences for Lifelong Learning*. Chugach recognizes ten continua as crucial for life after graduation. School to workplace programming identifies key skills for the worksites in a specific community.

This lack of consensus is an example of how different competency based learning is from the Taylorian "one best way" of curriculum-driven instruction. The key competencies for graduation are likely to be different in varied communities based on job opportunities, cultural differences, and the values of varied communities or families. The key competencies are likely to change with time as information, technology, economic factors, and shifts in patterns of affluence occur.

Time-based measures were appropriate in their day, but they are not now when we know more about how people learn and we have access to technology that can help us accommodate different styles and paces of learning. As we move to online learning and learning that combines classroom and online learning, time-based measures will increasingly frustrate our attempts to provide learning experiences that lead to achievement and the pursuit of postsecondary education that our modern world requires. Another basic assumption is the inflexible way we organize students into age-determined groups, structure separate academic disciplines, organize learning into classes of roughly equal size with all the students in a particular class receiving the same content at the same pace, and keep these groups in place all year . . .

Technology can facilitate implementation of such a competency-based approach to education.

—National Education Technology Plan
(US Department of Education, 2010)

We are at the beginning stages of developing competency based learning systems with a focus on getting ready for life after high school. In spite of the incredible stranglehold curriculum-driven instruction has over most of our schools, innovators are finding ways to develop competency based systems to meet the needs of their students.

Moving forward, there are so many exciting competency based questions to consider:

- ◆ In your district or community, what are the crucial outcomes that will help young men and women become ready to live and work in our changing world?
- ◆ Should we create course-based or life skill-based outcomes?
- ◆ How do we measure competency for these crucial outcomes?

- ◆ How do we create specific pathways toward these competencies and make each step clear and measureable?
- ◆ How do we train teachers to know their students learning needs and become facilitators of learning and development?
- ◆ How do we change a system that for more than a century has been designed to cover, test, and sort into a system that helps every student develop the skills to be an effective worker, learner, and citizen?

22
Competency Based Learning in Elementary and Preschools

Historically, preschool and elementary educators have deeply appreciated the importance of educating the whole child. They have demonstrated awareness of the importance of sensory-motor skills and social-emotional skills. They have dedicated time and energy to relationship building, establishing a secure environment within the classroom, and practiced consistent classroom routines. Experienced early childhood educators have an understanding of the need to give instruction that offers students "just enough" challenge but never so much that students become disengaged from learning.

But the curriculum-driven juggernaut of the last few decades has caused many schools to demand that early childhood and upper elementary classrooms maintain the "rigorous" pace of instruction that ensures coverage of every grade level content standard. As a result, many teachers have stepped away from instruction that better matches the needs of students, from giving attention to meeting the needs of the whole child, and from building a culture of trust and learning in the classroom.

Without a system in place to protect the development of crucial outcomes, many early childhood and elementary

> programs have become just another place where children race through content.

In the process of trying to cover more content, we have trivialized deep understanding of essential content and skills and forgotten the importance of nurturing the whole child. In many schools, early childhood and upper elementary educators have succumbed to institutional pressures and surrendered to pacing guides and one-size-fits-all instructional programs. During the vulnerable early childhood learning years, the effects of pushing kids into patterns of learning frustration are unconscionable.

It is widely understood that by the end of third grade we can predict long-term learning outcomes for individual students with astounding accuracy (Annie E. Casey Foundation, 2010; Hernandez, 2011; Sornson, 2012b; Snow et al., 1998; Torgeson, 1998; Torgeson, 2002). Yet in most schools/districts/states there has been no identification of and no system of tracking progress toward the crucial competencies that are the foundation for a lifetime of learning. Nonetheless, in every state and every community there are thoughtful educators lurking, waiting, and watching for the opportunity to give young students the basic learning and social skills they need.

> Long-term learning success can be predicted by the end of third grade. Building a competency based early learning initiative does not focus on job readiness skills. Instead, early childhood educators focus on the skills, concepts, and habits that allow children to become confident, skilled, motivated learners for life.

In Kennewick, Washington, district staff identified a sequence of skill levels for the development of K-2 language arts skills including phonemic awareness, phonics, accuracy, fluency, and comprehension. As reported in *Annual Growth for All Students, Catch Up Growth for Those Who Are Behind* (Fielding, Kerr, & Rosier 2007), progress in these aspects of literacy development was carefully monitored, and students were then given instruction and practice time for each skill until it was mastered. The Kennewick Schools are often cited as a model for Response to Intervention (RTI), which is conceptually a system for providing instruction to match the needs of each student and use systematic measurement of progress to make decisions about adjusting instruction.

RTI was identified in the 1997 Individuals with Disabilities Education Act as an alternative to using the severe discrepancy analysis to qualify for eligibility as an LD student, with the hope that early, diagnostic, explicit, and systematic interventions could help eliminate difficulties before they become entrenched. Without clear standards for implementation, RTI initiatives vary widely in form and efficacy.

Successful RTI initiatives follow the principles of competency based learning by identifying a manageable set of crucial outcomes to be the focus of on-going assessment, gauging the learning needs of students to determine skill levels and readiness for instruction, developing an instructional plan, and monitoring progress toward essential outcomes. While RTI initiatives typically focus on at-risk students, competency based learning initiatives are designed to address the needs of all students.

> Competency based early childhood and elementary educators are focused on the front end of the learning process, including the timely development of language skills, literacy, numeracy, sensory-motor, socio-emotional, and self-regulation skills.

Timber Ridge (Grades 3–8) and Clover Ridge Schools (K-2) in Albany, Oregon, have implemented standards-based instruction that includes a K-8 scope and sequence, explicit learning objectives, multi-age and subject integration, a personalized approach to learning, and a proficiency-based report card.

The Maine School Administrative District 15 has developed Learning Target Maps for the elementary through high school sequence of skills in English language arts, math, science, social studies, guidance, health-physical education, music, technology and engineering, visual arts, and world language.

The Re-Inventing Schools Coalition (RISC) was established in 2002, based on the model that had been developed in the Chugach School District, and has worked to develop competency based systems in over 30 districts. Among these is Adams County School District 50, which decided to introduce competency based learning at the elementary level, believing that a systemic approach would reduce the frustration of older students who had not developed competencies required for graduation. In the fall of 2009, Adams 50 began its conversion to standards-based education. Adams has replaced grades with Levels 1–10 that incorporate standards from elementary school through high school graduation. Staff are working to develop standards for proficiency, assessment, and improving instruction. They are working with Educate to create an information system to track student progression.

The Early Learning Foundation was established in 2001 and uses the *Essential Skill Inventories, Preschool through Grade 3*, (Sornson, 2012a) as its competency based framework during the early childhood years. Simpson County Schools in Mississippi and the Huron Schools, Bedford Public Schools, and Morenci Area Schools in Michigan use the K-3 inventories to update progress and use proficiency-based report cards, while several preschools in Michigan, Mississippi, and Belize use the *Preschool Essential Skills Inventory* with three- and four-year-old students.

Rather than focusing on literacy-only skills, the inventories include a set of crucial skills in all the domains of early childhood, including oral language, literacy, phonologic skills, numeracy, sensory-motor skills, behavior, and self-regulation. This reflects the belief that these are interrelated systems, that each domain is crucial for long-term learning success and is an example of whole-child accountability. While grade level competencies set the framework for minimum expected outcomes, teachers are trained to focus on outcomes from a previous grade level or a more advanced level as needed. By systematically updating data on the inventory, teachers become trained to use observational assessment and to embed formative assessment into the design of instruction.

Simpson Central School, a K-8 school, was the pilot for the *Essential Skill Inventories* in Simpson County, and began implementation of this competency model in 2008–09. They began with implementation in kindergarten, and gradually phased in first and second grade. Staff learned to:

- ◆ Clearly identify essential learning outcomes in all the domains of early childhood;
- ◆ Use systematic assessment to determine the readiness levels of students in relation to essential outcomes;
- ◆ Offer informed instruction and carefully monitor progress until these skills/objectives are deeply understood (competency);
- ◆ Advance students to higher-level work upon demonstration of mastery.

The district aligned report cards with the inventories, which encouraged staff to help parents understand the concept of crucial learning outcomes and to see more specifically what students were being asked to learn well. As part of an evaluation of improved teacher behaviors based on the use of this competency based learning model, teachers reported significant improvements in their teaching skills and behaviors associated with early learning success (Sornson, 2015). In 2007–08, before beginning this process, 37 percent of Simpson Central third graders scored at proficient or above on the state's reading tests, and 59 percent did so in math. In 2013–14, student outcomes had improved to almost 64 percent in reading and just over 86 percent in math (Sornson & Davis, 2013). At the beginning of the 2014–15 school year, Simpson Central School was rated as a Mississippi "A" level school, an extraordinary achievement for a high-poverty school. Teachers often refer to the essential skills as the "core of the core," and the district's goal is for 90 percent of primary students to reach or exceed competency in every grade level essential skill.

The digital revolution has not been lost on developers of early childhood learning products. Learning games, language and reading programs, math learning systems, digital home schooling models, video-game learning environments, digital learning with social networking, and more are part of the landscape of products for sale. Increasingly, toy, media, and product producers are exploring the early childhood learning market. The types and uses of technology in early childhood programs have expanded to include computers, tablets, e-books, mobile devices, handheld gaming devices, digital cameras and video camcorders, electronic toys, multimedia players for music and videos, digital audio recorders, interactive whiteboards, software applications, the Internet, streaming media, and more.

Everyone from the largest international education materials producers to small teams of app producers are looking for a portion of this digital learning market and building in scaffolding, curriculum objectives, internal tracking of success, assessment of progress, diagnostic reports, and data management. Digital competency based learning programs for both home and school are available. Some technology producers, like Dr. Dan Yang, founder of VINCI Education and the VINCI Virtual School, see systematic digital early childhood learning systems as a vehicle for closing the achievement gap and maximizing development in the early years.

Others express concern with the overuse of technology, the lack of interactive language, social, and physical experience, and the lack of hands on parent and caregiver involvement in the learning of young children. Thoughtful use of digital learning systems, blended systems, and technology to track progress along the pathways to major competencies in life is inevitable.

While digital options are increasingly available, some early learning skills require hands-on and three-dimensional learning. The *Essential Math Skills* (Sornson, 2014) offers a sequence of 29 preschool to Grade 3 math skills that are at the core of number sense and deep understanding of early math. A menu of hands-on or movement-based activities for each skill is suggested for each skill, but teachers and parents are encouraged to develop variations or additional activities.

This pathway to early math competency is not intended to be a lesson-by-lesson, one-size-fits-all learning program. Instead, it is a guide to help teachers track progress toward competency for each student while providing many activity options for instruction in small groups, activity centers, or individualized learning. Unlike a digital program that adjusts the task for you, this material puts teachers/parents in the role of instructional planner. Teachers are in charge of assessing student readiness, picking appropriate activities, monitoring progress, allowing more practice time or moving students forward to higher levels of challenge. With proficiency in these 29 math skills, students deeply understand and can apply basic number concepts and are prepared for more advanced traditional or digital learning math learning opportunities.

It is just as important to develop high-quality pathways to competency during the early learning years as at any other level. These are the foundational years, in which patterns of success, love of learning, and habits of mind are developed. These are the years during which the cover, test, sort educational model does the greatest harm. If we can help children develop solid basic skills while falling in love with learning, we will have improved the lives of our children and the future of our society.

The continued use of a coverage-driven model of learning for young children is causing many children to become discouraged and disengaged from learning. Poor or otherwise disadvantaged children pay an inordinately heavy cost. These kids are more likely to struggle to keep up with the pace of instruction, far more likely to become unsuccessful learners, and in time they are far more likely to end up with low-skill, low-wage jobs. If we ever honestly hope to level the playing field and give all children an opportunity to succeed in the information society, it will require a transition from one-size-fits-all instruction to a new model based on respect for the differences among us and the inherent potential in us all.

The transition to a competency model allows us to systematically offer every child the opportunity to become a lifelong learner. Moving to a competency based model allows us to consider the needs of the whole child, in all the domains of early childhood, including oral language, literacy, phonologic skills, numeracy, sensory-motor skills, behavior, and self-regulation.

In the competency based early learning environments of the future, pathways to success will be built with explicit and measureable learning objectives rather than long lists of things to race through so they are covered. Students will advance upon mastery, not be pushed along with the class without considering readiness. Assessment will be primarily formative, its purpose being to help the teacher know how to adjust instruction, rather than judging and comparing kids with grades.

Competency based learning systems at the preschool and elementary school levels have the potential to give far more students a chance to become successful learners for life. Identifying essential early learning outcomes, and building pathways to help children achieve these outcomes at their own rate of readiness, is the challenge and the opportunity of our time.

23

Teacher Education
Building Pathways to Skills That Matter

The enthusiastic attention given to competency based learning in some education sectors has not yet been matched by our teacher education programs. Credits based on seat time continue to be the way to earn teaching degrees. Because of a general mistrust of the quality of skills associated with teacher education program completion, most states also require candidates to pass a standardized test (such as the Praxis Exam, the National Evaluation Series, or the Professional Readiness Examination) for licensure.

Requirements for teacher certification vary on a state-by-state basis. Some states have specific credit and course requirements, while others allow state approved teacher education programs to set the standards for their institution. No states have yet established clear competencies, replacing traditional credit requirements, which would describe what you must know and be able to do as a prerequisite for teaching.

The CEU system used for continued teacher and administrator certification is a vivid example of our reliance on the time-based model.

In Michigan, 150 State Continuing Education Clock Hours (SCECHs) within three years allows you to renew your provisional certificate. In New York, to maintain a professional certificate a teacher can complete 175 hours of professional development every five years. In California, licenses can be renewed without verification of any professional development hours, although districts are required to offer a program of professional development of at least eighteen hours. In Oklahoma, 75 clock hours over a five year period allows you to renew your professional certificate.

A warm body can earn CEUs. If you are present and remember to sign in and sign out, you earn your contact hours. The quality of instruction is not considered. Learning outcomes are not considered. Application of learning is not considered.

The National Board for Professional Teaching Standards stands out as an exception to the continued emphasis on seat time and credits and was among the first voices for setting standards for teacher competency. This organization has developed standards for NBPTS certification in 25 certificate areas such as elementary art, high school English language arts, middle school math, etc. Experienced educators voluntarily seeking National Board certification go through a rigorous process to demonstrate their capacity to meet or exceed the standards. Since 1987, more than 110,000 teachers in the United States have achieved certification.

The United Nations Educational, Scientific, and Cultural Organization (UNESCO) ICT-CST project, working with Microsoft, Intel, Cisco, the International Society for Technology in Education (ISTE), and the Virginia Polytechnic Institute and State University (Virginia Tech), has developed a matrix of skills to help educational policy-makers and curriculum-developers identify the skills teachers need to harness technology in the service of education. The projects' *ICT Competency Standards for Teachers, Implementation Guidelines* (United Nations Educational, Scientific and Cultural Organization, 2008) identifies specific learning objectives for teachers and a suggested standard for how this could be applied in the classroom for technology literacy, knowledge deepening, and knowledge creation.

The Buros Center for Testing (1990), working with the American Federation of Teachers, the National Council on Measurement in Education, and the National Education Association, developed *Standards for Teacher Competence in Educational Assessment of Students*. These standards call on educators to demonstrate skill at selecting, developing, applying, using, communicating, and evaluating student assessment information and student assessment practices.

- Teachers should be skilled in choosing assessment methods appropriate for instructional decisions;
- Teachers should be skilled in developing assessment methods appropriate for instructional decisions;
- The teacher should be skilled in administering, scoring, and interpreting the results of both externally-produced and teacher-produced assessment methods;
- Teachers should be skilled in using assessment results when making decisions about individual students, planning teaching, developing curriculum, and school improvement;
- Teachers should be skilled in developing valid pupil grading procedures that use pupil assessments;
- Teachers should be skilled in communicating assessment results to students, parents, other lay audiences, and other educators;
- Teachers should be skilled in recognizing unethical, illegal, and otherwise inappropriate assessment methods and uses of assessment information.

The International Association for K-12 Online Learning (iNACOL, 2014) has developed a framework of competencies for blended learning. *iNACOL Blended Learning Teacher Competency Framework* describes a set of competencies under the headings of Mindsets, Qualities, Adaptive Skills, and Technical Skills.

The Teacher Leadership Consortium has developed its *Teacher Leader Model Standards* (2014) to guide the preparation of experienced teachers to assume leadership roles. These standards describe a set of skills in seven domains, including:

- Fostering a collaborative culture to support educator development and student learning;
- Accessing and using research to improve practice and student learning;
- Promoting professional learning for continuous improvement;
- Facilitating improvements in instruction and student learning;
- Promoting the use of assessments and data for school and district improvement;
- Improving outreach and collaboration with families and community;
- Advocating for student learning and the profession.

The Council of Chief State School Officers (CCSSO) and its Interstate Teacher Assessment and Support Consortium (inTASC) have created the *Model Core Teaching Standards and Learning Progressions for Teachers 1.0* (CCSSO, 2013). These standards are described as the teaching competencies needed across all grade levels and subject areas for a transformed public education system. The CCSSO recommends ten standards and a learning progression for each standard:

- Standard #1: Learner Development. The teacher understands how learners grow and develop, recognizing that patterns of learning and development vary individually within and across the cognitive, linguistic, social, emotional, and physical areas, and designs and implements developmentally appropriate and challenging learning experiences.
- Standard #2: Learning Differences. The teacher uses understanding of individual differences and diverse cultures and communities to ensure inclusive learning environments that enable each learner to meet high standards.
- Standard #3: Learning Environments. The teacher works with others to create environments that support individual and collaborative learning and that encourage positive social interaction, active engagement in learning, and self-motivation.

◆ Standard #4: Content Knowledge. The teacher understands the central concepts, tools of inquiry, and structures of the discipline(s) he or she teaches and creates
learning experiences that make the discipline accessible
and meaningful for learners to assure mastery of the
content.

◆ Standard #5: Application of Content. The teacher understands how to connect concepts and use differing perspectives to engage learners in critical thinking, creativity,
and collaborative problem solving related to authentic
local and global issues.

◆ Standard #6: Assessment. The teacher understands
and uses multiple methods of assessment to engage
learners in their own growth, to monitor learner progress, and to guide the teacher's and learner's decision
making.

◆ Standard #7: Planning for Instruction. The teacher plans
instruction that supports every student in meeting rigorous learning goals by drawing upon knowledge of
content areas, curriculum, cross-disciplinary skills, and
pedagogy, as well as knowledge of learners and the community context.

◆ Standard #8: Instructional Strategies. The teacher understands and uses a variety of instructional strategies to
encourage learners to develop deep understanding of
content areas and their connections and to build skills to
apply knowledge in meaningful ways.

◆ Standard #9: Professional Learning and Ethical Practice.
The teacher engages in ongoing professional learning
and uses evidence to continually evaluate his/her practice, particularly the effects of his/her choices and actions
on others (learners, families, other professionals, and the
community), and adapts practice to meet the needs of
each learner.

◆ Standard #10: Leadership and Collaboration. The teacher
seeks appropriate leadership roles and opportunities to
take responsibility for student learning, to collaborate

with learners, families, colleagues, other school professionals, and community members to ensure learner growth, and to advance the profession.

The National Association of Elementary School Principals (2014) has called for principals to achieve six school leadership competencies in support of the development of high-quality early learning from age three to Grade 3. The framework for these Pre-K to Grade 3 administrative competencies includes:

◆ Embrace the Pre-K–3 Early Learning Continuum. Effective principals embrace a concept of high-quality early learning from age three to grade three as the foundation for children's developmental growth.

◆ Ensure Developmentally-Appropriate Teaching. Effective principals ensure quality teaching, supported by a system of standards, and developmentally appropriate curriculum and assessments that work together to help foster children's learning and growth.

◆ Provide Personalized, Blended Learning Environments. Effective principals provide welcoming, collaborative learning environments that support personalized learning, including the effective use of technology.

◆ Use Multiple Measures to Guide Growth in Student Learning. Effective principals use multiple measures to assess student progress and support student learning growth.

◆ Build Professional Capacity Across the Learning Community. Effective principals build collaborative working environments that support the professional growth of all who work in them.

◆ Make Your School a Hub of Pre-K–3 Learning for Families and Communities. Effective principals work with families, prekindergarten programs, and community organizations to build strong Pre-K–3 linkages. Effective principals work with families, pre-kindergarten programs, and community organizations to build strong Pre-K–3 linkages.

These examples reflect the beginning stages of considering and then building competency frameworks for educator development. Under the curriculum-driven CTS model, the expectation for teachers was simple: manage behavior and cover the content. Without a sense of urgency that all students succeed, the coverage-based teacher training model sufficed. Finding the best teacher candidates, ensuring that each teacher-in-training developed a set of crucial skills, and then offering continued on-the-job training to reach higher levels of skill and professionalism was not considered essential.

Some schools are not waiting for state or university teacher training requirements to change and have already taken steps to more specifically define the competencies they want. In most school districts, these standards or competencies are built into the teacher evaluation systems and may not yet be designed for systematically working to develop the crucial competencies desired in their staff. But there is opportunity for innovation among schools who can more specifically define what they want teachers to know and be able to do, create personalized learning pathways, and set standards for demonstration of competence in every crucial teaching skill.

The Summit Public Schools is one example of a district that has blended evaluation with planned learning to improve teacher skills. Summit is a system of seven charter middle and high schools headquartered in Redwood City, California, which measures teachers using seven categories: assessment, content, curriculum, instruction, knowing learners and learning, leadership, and mentoring. Depending on how well they can demonstrate their expertise in each of these areas, teachers are placed at one of four levels: basic, proficient, highly proficient, and expert. Every teacher participates in at least 40 days of professional development per year, which is designed to mirror the self-directed learning model used with Summit students.

As we realize the importance of helping lots more students become successful lifelong learners, we have reached a tipping point. Failure to help children learn well inflicts incredible costs both to students and to society. The efficacy of instruction matters. We have reached the point at which we are beginning to realize that the skills of our teachers are just as important as the skills of nurses, doctors, electricians, tech workers, plumbers, and accountants. Teacher competency matters.

Competency based teacher education requires a new starting point. Instead of preparing a curriculum or course plan by identifying content and reading, a competency based teacher development programs begin by identifying essential competencies. These guide the selection of readings, projects, assignments, and assessments to support crucial learning. Teacher training institutions and/or states are challenged to:

♦ Develop a competency map for what teachers should know and be able to do. The map can be specific to your state/community's learning needs and the needs of differing roles within the education community. The crucial competencies must be spelled out clearly;

♦ Develop pathways to your crucial competencies, the steps that lead to your desired outcomes;

♦ Develop clear rubrics and reliable assessments of competency for each and every step along the pathway;

♦ Ensure that students are included in the development of personalized plans to develop each competency;

♦ Allow students to include learning goals that exceed competency in some areas.

♦ Assess the learning needs of teacher candidates;

♦ Develop training systems that include personalization based on the learning needs of each student;

♦ Develop cohort and online support systems for developing educators;

♦ Identify existing resources that match the identified learning needs;

♦ Find or develop instructional options that are missing from present-day teacher education programs;

♦ Use demonstrated competence rather than courses and credits to certify teachers;

♦ Work with school districts and other institutions to develop post-certification training programs to support educators who wish to achieve higher levels of competency.

24

Distracted by the Debate over What to Cover

The Common Core State Standards are not a competency framework. They offer a framework for coverage, describing those areas of content that are recommended for inclusion in the curriculum. The Texas Essential Knowledge and Skills standards (TEKS) are a coverage framework, as are the Indiana Academic Standards, and every other set of state grade-level content standards. Across the nation, these "standards" as we know them are a list of things to cover or include in the instruction, offering a general map of what can be taught at the different grades and ages.

There is a contentious debate about the use of the CCSS raging across the nation. Indeed, most states promised to adopt the CCSS before they were completed in their final form, without having any opportunity to carefully review them, as a prerequisite for applying to receive Race to the Top funding. States agreed to the idea of common standards without knowing all the details.

The debate has turned political, and some states have withdrawn their promise to use the Common Core State Standards or one of the two national summative tests developed to measure progress toward CCSS. Some objectors to the CCSS argue that the early math standards are not rigorous enough, that the early literacy standards are not developmentally appropriate for many children, that a liberal bias is included in the choice of English and social studies content expectations, or that the Massachusetts State Standards were more rigorous and should be used as the national standard. These are among the many questions that could be debated, and there are an infinite number of opinions regarding what should be included in K-12 instructional content.

> If it was possible to tinker with our curriculum-driven instructional design to get far greater outcomes, all these CCSS related questions and objections might deserve careful attention. But if the Cover Test Sort design is inadequate to meet the needs of students in the 21st century, it may be time to quell the rancor over CCSS and figure out how to move quickly toward a competency based learning model.

More than a hundred years after Frederick Winslow Taylor described his management principles in the book *The Principles of Scientific Management* (Taylor, 1911), today's CCSS debate demonstrates how we continue to search for "the one best way" of standardized instruction. *"What are we going to cover, and how are we going to test it?"* are questions from the old Prussian, Taylorized, curriculum-driven, summative test-driven school model, which has failed us for far too long and is now experiencing its death throes.

As we begin down the road of developing systems based on competency based learning, let's hope that no one claims to have "the one best way" for a very long time. There is so much to learn about competency based learning models that work. There are many differing ideas of what we want a high school graduate to know and be able to do. We've barely begun the development of pathways to competency and, arguably, are beginning to see that there can be multiple pathways to competency. School to work initiatives are growing but will change each decade with the evolving demands of the workplace. Higher education has just begun to compete for students in a competency driven environment. Technology gives us opportunities for individualized learning, digital learning, free learning options, and blended learning. As competency based learning options become available, families can also play a greater role in the development of their children.

From now on, learning is for life. Individuals will learn at home, at school, online, and in groups throughout their lives as a condition for being productive and well-informed men and women. The old top-down cover-test-sort model cannot serve the needs of people who need personalized lifelong learning. Out of habit, some educators will continue to tinker with the curriculum-driven system and fight about what should be "covered." But those systems are failing and will soon be gone, replaced by systems and individuals who create pathways to competency.

25

Defending Curriculum-Driven Instruction

For many years, we've equated being a teacher with preparing good lesson plans and then delivering them well. We've been asked to turn in lesson plans every week, noting the state or national standards covered in each plan. We've worked on committees to develop pacing guides and district quarterly assessments to ensure that everyone is keeping up with the plan for coverage. Our curriculum maps have been remodeled to fit the CCSS. We've purchased learning programs and textbooks that claim to cover all the standards, if only we can keep up the pace of instruction. We're up to our ears in alligators. Leave us alone!

> When people are ready to, they change. They never do it before then, and sometimes they die before they get around to it. You can't make them change if they don't want to, just like when they do want to, you can't stop them.
> —Andy Warhol

The implementation of competency based learning will elicit resistance for all the usual human reasons. Here are just a few:

Safety

There is safety in the familiar. With our years of training and well-refined skills in curriculum-driven instruction, there is an element of danger in changing to a model in which the demands and expectations are different.

Mental Models

As children, we developed a mental model of what it is to be a teacher. Sister Mary Bruno, Mr. Mitrano, and Mrs. Larsen were inspiring representations of what it means to be a teacher. Within the stand and deliver model of instruction, they were brilliant models. It is hard to change our cognitive representations of learning and teaching.

Comfortable Routines

On Sunday night, we sit on the porch and write lessons for the week. For years, this has been the routine. And now someone wants us to prepare learning plans based on identified, crucial outcomes, knowing our students, providing instruction matched to their specific learning needs, also providing some group activities for exploration, exposure, and general knowledge. The old way was simpler, more familiar, and more comfortable.

Effort

Years ago, we developed high-quality lesson plans, and then we refined them over the years so that all the new content expectations were also being covered. We have study guides and tests all prepared that go along with those lessons. Now you want us to become the guide on the side instead of the sage on the stage. You want us to abandon the lesson plans on which we have spent countless hours.

Limitations on Personal Responsibility

To some degree, we all put limits on taking personal responsibility for another person's effort and learning. Competency based learning creates the clear expectation that crucial outcomes must be learned to deep understanding and application. Teachers might be fearful of being held to that standard. This is partly because they have not fully realized that if students have clear learning goals and are given instruction at their level, with the understanding that competency precedes moving on, students' ownership of their own learning will be vastly improved.

One More Thing

Many experienced teachers have seen the new educational fads coming around every few years. They might easily assume that CBL is just another fad and will fade away in a few years like so many other programs or buzzwords.

Perceived Status

Some staff members have worked for years to gain a sense of respect from their colleagues or in their community. Any significant change initiative threatens familiar roles and the perception of status.

Lack of Skills and Training

Please don't put me in the pilot's seat of an airplane without first giving me quality training. Educators who do not understand instructional match, have seldom used formative assessment, and are not yet familiar with systematic observational assessment will be justly afraid of the demands of competency based learning.

Lack of Trust

When educators feel they cannot trust each other or key school decision makers, it is hard to accept change. When you are in a fear-based organizational culture, you resist new ideas. Trust is a necessary component for optimal thinking, listening, collaboration, and problem-solving.

Good Excuses for Low Expectations

Competency requires clear, high standards for crucial learning outcomes. Some teachers who are used to the coverage model will find ways to excuse low performance and try to certify students as competent even when they are not. *He tries so hard. She brought in brownies for extra credit. Her parents are such nice people.* Likewise, administrators want their teachers to be successful, and some will find ways to pretend that consistent, formative assessment or high-quality, differentiated instruction are happening in the classroom.

We Are Way Too Busy

When we are asked to do something new, difficult, or not yet fully understood, some folks will find ways to avoid it. Just as we fill up our day with busy work when we are avoiding some chore at home, some educators will find that the day was far too busy to get around to data collection, individual planning, or other important aspects of CBL.

The Kids Love Me Just as I Am

There are many reasons to justify resisting change, and this one is a classic. Teachers who have managed to somehow get kids to love them even while they are delivering one-size-fits-all instruction can certainly get kids to love them when they start to deliver high-quality, competency based instruction.

> At every crossway on the road that leads to the future, each progressive spirit is opposed by a thousand men assigned to guard the past.
> —Nobel laureate Maurice Maeterlinck (1911)

Our School Is Doing Fine without CBL

In most cases, schools look for new ideas only when they see a need. Chugach, New Hampshire, and Simpson County Schools wanted to vastly improve their outcomes. Occasionally, a successful school with some extraordinary leaders (including teacher leaders) will look for a better way. Some schools will resist CBL by clinging to the belief that they are already doing everything that can possibly be done to serve their students.

We Are Already Doing Competency

Some school leaders have the most amazing capacity to believe/say they are already doing every new thing that comes along in the world of education. Whole child learning, differentiated instruction, response to intervention, constructivism, nature learning, learning styles, multiple intelligences, personalized learning, blended learning, home-school connections, scaffolding, early intervention, socio-emotional learning, character development, and competency. *Oh yes, we are already doing that.*

Money and Power

Competency based learning offers efficiencies that could reduce some of the unnecessary costs of our highly bureaucratic and educationally inept systems. Nonetheless, there are powerful financial and political interests that will protect the status quo.

One-size-fits-all assessment systems, textbooks, workbooks, and other learning materials won't stand the test of a competency-driven system. They will need to be adapted to the different design needs of a competency-driven system. The designers, distributors, and monitors of rigid pacing guides will abhor the individualization that comes with competency systems. Politicians and bureaucrats who favor overly simplistic, one-size-fits-all regulations will find a way to not understand the need for change towards a more effective, respectful, and joyful way of teaching and learning.

Change can be seen as both an opportunity and a crisis. For every teacher who embraces competency based learning as an opportunity to meet the needs of each student, there will be others who resist giving up familiar lessons plans and worksheets. For every administrator who has longed for a better way to create respectful environments for learning, and schools where teachers love to teach, there will be others who hold on to familiar patterns and do not want to do the challenging work of recreating systems of learning. For every politician who actually reads the research and understands how much we need thoughtful planning toward a more effective system of training our children to compete in a global society, there will be others who cling to political posturing from the past. For every entrepreneur who sees the opportunity to develop new learning products and systems, there are huge international companies with political clout who are trying to hold onto market share.

> The logistics of making the change to competency based learning are not as daunting as they might seem.

The model is here, all around us. Resources, the experience of trailbreakers, and expert guidance are available. Every principle of good teaching and learning supports the practice of competency based learning. Teachers and administrators urgently want to be part of a system that succeeds for kids, in which they get to be professionals and work within a respectful and collaborative environment. Parents and community leaders are clamoring for the changes that will help their children be intellectually and emotionally ready to succeed in the modern world.

Resistance is a natural part of change, within individuals and within our business, political, and educational systems. We can't wish it gone or push it away. With resolve and compassion, those who embrace the opportunity to create competency based learning systems can overcome these predictable patterns and build learning systems in which the highest standards for learning, teaching, empathy, and character flourish.

26

Transitioning from Curriculum-Driven to Competency Based Learning

Those schools, school districts, colleges, preschools, publishers, technology innovators, thinkers, and community members who choose to lead the transformation towards competency based learning systems will face many challenges. We are redesigning an airplane that is in flight. We can't shut down the schools and just study all this for a few years. There are millions of young men and women in the process of being educated today. None of that stops. No timeouts. The transformation to competency based learning will emerge from the curriculum-driven systems in which we now operate.

For those who are ready to innovate, this will be the most exciting time in the history of education. We have barely scratched the surface of the potential for human learning. Decades of discovery and transformation lie ahead. We need thoughtful educators, parents, and community leaders to create pathways to knowledge and competent skills that matter.

New systems of defining the expertise and instruction needed for highly skilled jobs are waiting to be developed. The skills needed for high school completion must be redefined and will likely look different from place to place. The basic structure of high schools will be reconsidered. It is unlikely that all students need to take the same courses or develop the same skill sets to be successful in the world.

The foundation skills needed in the early years of learning have only recently been mapped, and the many ways to help children develop these skills will be reconceptualized by innovative educators and parents. One-size-fits-all learning programs are unlikely to persist, and a new generation of Montessoris, Steiners, Vygotskys, Ericksons, and Deweys will lead us to consider better systems of learning to meet the needs of modern learners.

Digital, blended, hands-on, and socially interactive learning systems will be developed to bring learning alive for more students, to extend learning so that learning is truly possible anywhere, anytime, and at any pace.

The excitement of creating new systems may bring back those gifted individuals we so desperately need to public and private education. Be an educator. From the ashes of decades of school reform failure will emerge the Phoenix of education systems that bring learning alive for our children.

> Start by doing what's necessary; then do what's possible; and suddenly you are doing the impossible.
> —St. Francis of Assisi

It is already happening. From Alaska to New Hampshire, from universities to preschools, there is recognition that competency matters and that we can design systems that allow far more students to become successful learners for life. The years of transition ahead of us will be filled with innovation and experimentation, mistakes and discoveries. Consider these ideas as you create high-quality, competency based systems in your school or community.

Take time for preliminary planning, knowing that the process of transformation will last for years. Too often in education we adopt the newest standards without having an opportunity to even read them or embrace a new instructional program without carefully planning for the rollout challenges. Pick thoughtful contributors to this study process who represent all stakeholder groups and allow them to do meaningful work. Examine the change from as many different perspectives as possible. Build a clear consensus around the need for transformation.

Pick a point of beginning, whether it is high school graduation requirements, certificate completion competencies, or early childhood essential outcomes. Decide on the competencies or outcomes that are essential, and make sure these are described precisely. Coverage standards can be vague; competencies must be crystal clear.

Design the competency based learning architecture, Version 1.0. This design starts with:

- ◆ Clear competencies that articulate exactly what students need to know and be able to do;
- ◆ Specific steps along the pathways to competency;
- ◆ Rubrics that describe the standards for proficiency/competency/mastery at each step;
- ◆ The development, purchase, and/or adaptation of an instructional plan (curriculum) and instructional materials organized around the competencies;
- ◆ Assessment systems (formative and summative) that are consistent and reliable;
- ◆ The role of technology for instruction;
- ◆ The role of technology for assessment;
- ◆ Opportunities for students to help choose learning goals above minimum expectations;
- ◆ The role of the student to help design pathways to competency that match interests and learning style;

 ◆ Home-school partnerships that allow parent input and
   the development of learning plans and participation in
   the learning process;
 ◆ Systems to communicate progress toward competency in
   the required and chosen learning goals;
 ◆ Short term and on-going staff and community training
   needs.

Develop a three- to five-year plan for implementation. Set
milestones to track progress in each essential element of the
plan, and create systems to track advancement toward each
milestone. If it is possible, plan on implementing change in
phases. This will allow you to work out any problems that
emerge in the process.

Form a transition team to monitor and ensure progress.
Recruit stakeholders from all parts of the system/school. Teacher
leaders and other employees who have the respect of the staff
should be part of the transition team. Gather support for the
change from all school leaders, including those who are not part
of management. Make sure that the initiative is not seen as the
product of a small group of visionaries, and that it is not seen
as one more thing that will disappear in two to three years.

**Begin training staff long before implementing the prelimi-
nary roll out.** You can choose to train only those employees that
will be affected first, or you can train all employees that will
eventually be affected. Remember that training is more than
"coverage." Helping staff develop competency in all the skills
needed for CBL will include significant training over time.

Develop teacher leaders. Individual coaching and peer mentoring models can be helpful with reluctant staff members who
might procrastinate, miss deadlines, or avoid the significant
learning needed to become a successful competency based
instructor. Working side-by-side with a peer who can encourage,
clarify, and help them keep pace with the change process can
make individuals feel more like a part of a team.

Become a learning organization. Most educators will need
to develop new skills to enable them to succeed in this new

model of learning. Some of these skills include, but are not limited to:

♦ Aligning instruction to the explicit, measurable learning objectives that make up the pathway to competency;
♦ Providing timely, differentiated support to students based on individual learning needs, moving each student along an individual learning pathway at a sufficient pace to achieve essential learning goals;
♦ Using formative and summative assessments to regularly assess student progress;
♦ Developing and implementing performance-based formative and summative assessments with high validity and reliability;
♦ Collaborating with other staff members for the development and implementation of assessment and instructional plans;
♦ Using data on individual student learning in a timely, ongoing manner to inform instruction and support student progress to competency;
♦ Supporting development of the whole child/student including social and emotional competencies;
♦ Designing and managing personalized instruction using technology, blended or online learning, and other options;
♦ Working with students to get input on student learning goals or a plan for pathways to competency;
♦ Working with parents to build strong partnerships supporting the development of competency.

Clear the obstacles to implementation. Identify employees or community leaders that may cause obstacles to the transition and work with them. Identify resource issues that could interfere with your plan's implementation or success.

Plan the transition. Allow the transition team to give input before crafting a final implementation plan. Create a comprehensive plan detailing how the transition will take place, how it will affect each group of stakeholders, and the timetable for the change. The transition team should present the plan to the school and community with confidence, and the plan must be clear enough for everyone to understand the vision.

Put the transition plan on paper so everyone knows the blueprint for change. This plan should explain why the change is being made and what the school will look like when the transition is complete.

Proceed one step at a time. While many of us may be frustrated by the slow pace of change, the creation of a competency based learning system must be done well. Rushing through the plan sounds a lot like rushing through instruction. Take your time, help people along, ensure understanding, experiment, innovate, learn from your mistakes, and enjoy the process of creating meaningful change that will last.

27

Informed Instruction Leads to Competency, Part Two

Curriculum-driven instruction is based on one set of concepts or thought patterns. Teachers cover material at a specified pace. Tests are given to know how well students understood the material. The teacher then moves forward to cover new material. Successful students keep up with the pace of instruction. Successful students advance toward higher levels of learning. Rigor is related to covering more content. Less successful students are screened into classes and careers that require less learning. A large majority of students will fall into patterns of disengagement from learning. Education experts develop content expectations, which teachers are expected to cover. District summative assessment systems, digital assessment systems, and state assessment systems are in place to ensure coverage and judge the success of schools and teachers.

> Cover, test, and sort worked well enough in the 19th and early 20th centuries. But in today's world, it is a greater burden to be an unsuccessful learner, as this leads to a life of low-skill and low-wage employment opportunities.

Competency based learning is driven by a different set of premises. Lifelong learning is an essential ingredient for personal, social, and economic success. People learn best when important instruction is given at the student's readiness level. Students should move on to higher levels of learning when they are fully ready. Essential learning outcomes must be clear and compelling. Pathways to competency show the steps that build up to high-level competencies. Instructors should know each student's level of readiness and deliver crucial instruction at that level. Children learn at different rates and in different ways. Given the necessary time and instruction, almost all students can achieve competency in important language, social-emotional, motor, literacy, and numeracy skills needed for a foundation of learning success. Given the necessary time and instruction, almost all students can advance along the pathways to competency that will allow them access to the job skills that can support personal success. Learning can occur anywhere, at any time of day, and at any pace.

> In a chronically leaking boat, energy devoted to changing vessels is more productive than energy devoted to patching leaks.
>
> —Warren Buffett

Learning models are informed by their premises. No reasonable person argues that all students learn in the same way or at the same pace. Yet rigid pacing guides abound in our schools. It is part of the basic paradigm, the thought pattern for how we do things, the patterns we accept without careful scrutiny.

When Vygotsky, Betts, Gickling, or Burns described the importance of *instructional match*, educators understood its importance. But nothing much changed. When Schmoker and Marzano called for *standards that are clear, not confusing; essential, not exhaustive*, we wholeheartedly agreed. But our patterns of instruction persisted. When DuFour and Eaker articulated the first key question of PLCs, *What do we expect students to learn*, we celebrated this wisdom. But again nothing changed. As John

Hattie urged us to *clarify what students must learn* as the first step for a successful learning strategy, we acknowledged this obvious truth, but most schools have not yet acted upon this research.

Throughout this book, we have explored a set of simple ideas about teaching and learning. Identify crucial learning outcomes. Find out what your students can do and what they are ready to learn. For crucial outcomes, plan instruction based on a student's instructional level. Deliver informed instruction for as long as it takes until the outcome is well learned. Move students along when they are ready. Competency matters.

Despite the research, most educators go to work and give great energy to perpetuating the old model. We cling to what we know. The boat is leaking, and we know how patch leaks, and we do so with vigor. We may be so busy patching that we never look up long enough to see that a new vessel is there, waiting to be discovered.

The CTS educational model was informed by long lists of grade level content standards and pacing guides. Teachers were asked to race through nonviable content at breakneck speed and then judged to have failed when students were not able to successfully perform on summative assessments. With kids struggling and teachers struggling, there was too much failure to go around.

A new model is emerging. It is designed with an understanding of the importance of learning success. It is built to help students achieve clear and crucial learning goals. It is informed by a solid understanding of a child's readiness for learning and by the commitment to give students what they need at their instructional level for as long as it takes. Its architecture includes pathways to competency, sometimes different for one student than another. In this model, learning is for life and must be based on the joyful engagement of the learner.

28

Conclusion

The Spirit of Transformation

One-size-fits-all education systems no longer serve the needs of individuals or of society. While transformational change is occurring in science and technology, and while new ideas and new business models emerge at unprecedented rates, our institutions of education have been astonishingly successful at resisting change, until now. In a world of innovation and information, we are responsible to help our children develop the foundation skills, the habits of learning, and a powerful understanding that they can be learners for life.

Those of us who are educators, parents, and community leaders have the information, tools, and opportunity to create an educational process that works for many more students, a process that respects diversity, embraces personalization, and continuously improves.

We live in an era of transformation. At no time in history has there been more scientific inquiry, information, technology, freedom, and capacity for change. In the past hundred years, change has become the constant, affecting every aspect of the way we live and work.

At Kitty Hawk, North Carolina, on December 17, 1903, the Wright brothers achieved the first sustained flight with a powered, controlled aircraft. Orville Wright was the pilot of the first flight of 120 feet in 12 seconds. In the fourth flight of the same day, Wilbur Wright flew 852 feet in 59 seconds. The age of air travel had begun, and human ingenuity is hard to restrain.

From those first precarious flights came an astonishing sequence of innovations. In less than 66 years, space flight accomplished the unimaginable. On July 20, 1969, Neil Armstrong and Buzz Aldrin became the first humans to step onto the surface of the moon. They spent about two and a half hours on the moon, rejoined Michael Collins on the command spacecraft that was in lunar orbit, and returned to Earth. We've begun to explore the unfathomable limits of space. Soon there will be manned visits to Mars.

Beginning in the mid-19th century, generations of woman suffrage supporters lectured, wrote, marched, lobbied, and practiced civil disobedience to secure the basic right to vote and run for office. What seemed like a radical idea to some became the law of the land, finally passed by Congress in 1919 and ratified on August 18, 1920. The transformation away from gender-based limitations has begun.

In the United States, slavery was legal in all thirteen colonies at the inception of our country. By 1850, there were 4 million slaves in our country. The Civil War effectively ended slavery, and the thirteenth amendment to the Constitution was formally approved in 1865. Even then, Jim Crow segregation laws limited access to schools and public facilities for many black Americans. Anti-miscegenation laws prohibited whites and blacks from marrying each other. Voting rights were limited in some states. Black servicemen often served in segregated units. Jackie Robinson joined the Brooklyn Dodgers in 1947, beginning a pattern of change in sports. In December 1955, Rosa Parks refused to go the back of the bus in Montgomery, Alabama. Not until 1968 did the Civil Rights Act ban discrimination in the sale and rental of homes. Discrimination based on race is now illegal.

As recently as the early 1980s, almost one third of the world's population lived in a totalitarian communist state, with strong government control over the economic, political, and personal lives of its citizens. Poland, East Germany, Czechoslovakia, Bulgaria, Romania, and Hungary began the exodus from this political system, and the Soviet Union dissolved in 1991. The People's Republic of China began its economic reforms in 1978 and has introduced market-based reforms since that time. The idea of an economy driven by totalitarian government edicts has been discredited.

> Focus on where you want to go, not on what you fear.
> —Anthony Robbins

Satellites roam our skies, bringing us information and entertainment. We talk to our phones, and they guide us turn by turn as we travel. The smartphone in your pocket has more computing power than the entire National Aeronautics and Space Administration (NASA) when astronauts completed the moon mission. We can search for information on any topic with astonishing speed. Diseases that once ravaged the planet have been eliminated or diminished. Many of us safely travel tens of thousands of miles through the air each year. We've mapped the human genome and discovered the human microbiome. Surely we have the capacity to personalize learning, track progress, and challenge students at the level that optimizes success.

The clamor for school reform over the last several decades has focused on reshaping lists of what to "cover" and using high stakes summative assessments to measure surface level learning and memory of facts. The curriculum-driven instructional model has generally gone unchallenged for over 150 years. But this age in which we live offers us the option to change.

> This is the age of transformation, unleashing the potential of men and women of every race and in every corner of the world, unleashing the power of technology and science, unleashing the power of learning.

Our challenges are great, but our consciousness, knowledge, skills, and technology have never been greater. Our capacity for change has never been greater. We can transcend the limitations of an education process that diminishes the learning outcomes of our children, punishes the poor, and fails to teach most students to develop the skills, habits, and character needed in the modern world.

Somewhere in Mississippi, a first grader receives reading instruction. His teacher knows exactly which skills he has already developed to competency and how to design instruction at just the right level of difficulty to keep him fully engaged. He loves school, and he loves learning.

In New Hampshire, a tenth grader has been slacking off in science. Just a few years ago, she might have earned a C and moved along, but her teachers don't do it that way anymore. She asks her teacher for a meeting, and they put together a plan for her to catch up on some of the science outcomes for which she has not yet developed competency.

A ten-year-old homeschooled student has fallen in love with math. After developing the essential early math skills using lots of hands on activities, she started to work using a digital math learning program. She's way ahead of age expectations and goes back and forth between her digital learning program, the Khan Academy, evening sessions with Dad, and her online support team to find challenges that are interesting.

In his second year of college, a young man has completed all but a few of the requirements for his bachelor's degree, along with three certificates of skill. Many of his credits were earned using a competency based program in his high school and local community college. This semester, he's preparing his resume and applying for jobs, and, with his competency profile, he is able to show prospective employers exactly which skills he has developed and is ready to use in the workplace.

A graduate level education student is reviewing her personal vision statement to help her develop her personal learning plan. After eight years of teaching, she has a more mature view of what she can accomplish. Soon she'll sit with a program planner, who will add this student's personal learning goals to the competency expectations for her advanced degree. Then they'll plan a learning program that supports the development of competency for every objective.

The transformation has begun. Learning and persistence are the currency of the future. Our children, and students of any age, deserve a thoughtful education system that recognizes individual learning needs and offers a clear pathway to the knowledge and skills they need.

Appendix 1

Organizational Self-Assessment for Readiness to Implement Competency Based Learning

Please reflect on the following statements, indicating how accurate this statement is for your organization. Rate 1 for low accuracy and up to 5 for high accuracy. Circle your response.

1 2 3 4 5   We have taken the time to study competency based learning and how it applies to our learning programs.

1 2 3 4 5   A leadership team comprised of committed school and community members has been identified.

1 2 3 4 5   A point of beginning for competency based learning has been identified.

1 2 3 4 5   A clear vision for where we hope to be in three to five years has been developed.

1 2 3 4 5   A comprehensive transition plan has been established.

1 2 3 4 5   Staff, administration, student, and community training needs have been identified.

1 2 3 4 5   Obstacles to implementation have been identified and considered.

1 2 3 4 5   Necessary resources to support transition activities are in place.

1 2 3 4 5   Our vision and first steps in transition are clear to all concerned.

Appendix 2

Resources for the Further Study of Competency Based Learning

Achieve is an independent, nonpartisan, nonprofit education reform organization working with states to raise academic standards and graduation requirements, improve assessments, and strengthen accountability.

> http://www.achieve.org/publications/advancing-competency-based-pathways-college-and-career-readiness

American Youth Policy Forum provides learning opportunities toward the development of effective youth and education policies. Their guiding principles include Student-Centered Learning, Advancement upon Mastery, Multiple Pathways to Success, and Creating Collaborative Systems that Support Youth.

> http://www.aypf.org/

Annie E. Casey Foundation is a private charitable organization dedicated to helping build better futures for disadvantaged children in the US. Their work focuses on strengthening families, building stronger communities, and education issues. They have been strong advocates for the importance of preschool through Grade 3 learning outcomes.

> http://www.aecf.org/

Bill and Melinda Gates Foundation's *Early Progress: Interim Research on Personalized Learning* found that although results varied considerably among the 23 schools in this study, two-thirds of them had statistically significant positive effects on students' math and reading scores on the Northwest Education Association's Measures of Academic Progress (MAP) assessments."

http://collegeready.gatesfoundation.org/sites/default/
files/Early%20Progress%20Interim%20Report%20on%20
Personalized%20Learning%20-%20Full%20Report.pdf

Carnegie Foundation for the Advancement of Teaching is a
US-based education policy and research center. It has conducted
research on the efficacy of the practice of Carnegie Units and
seat time to measure learning.
http://www.carnegiefoundation.org/?s=competency+based&
submit=go

Chugach School District, Alaska
http://www.chugachschools.com/pages/Chugach_School_
District
http://www.competencyworks.org/resources/how-
alaskas-chugach-district-changed-education-through-
performance-based-learning/

Clayton Christensen Institute for Disruptive Innovation is a
nonprofit, nonpartisan think tank dedicated to improving the
world through disruptive innovation. The theory of disruptive
innovation describes a process by which a product or service
transforms an existing market by introducing simplicity, conve-
nience, accessibility, and affordability.
http://www.christenseninstitute.org/our-mission/#sthash.
YRRfWSZD.dpuf
http://www.christenseninstitute.org/

Competency-Based Education Network (C-BEN), administered
by Public Agenda, is a group of regionally accredited colleges
and universities working together to address shared challenges
to designing, developing, and scaling competency-based degree
programs.
http://www.cael.org/what-we-do/competency-based-
education#sthash.gklbqi3e.dpuf

CompetencyWorks provides a variety of resources to help you understand competency education, including examples, policy, practice tips, and Issue Briefs.

    http://www.competencyworks.org/
    http://competencyworks.pbworks.com/w/page/
      66734498/Welcome%20to%20the%20Competency-
      Works%20Wiki

Council for Adult & Experiential Learning is a nonprofit that works within the higher education, public, and private sectors to help adult learners get the education and training they need. With funding from Lumina Foundation for Education, the Council for Adult and Experiential Learning (CAEL) offers postsecondary institutions training on competency-based education.

    http://www.cael.org/what-we-do/competency-based-
    education

Council of Chief State School Officers is a nonpartisan, nonprofit organization of public officials who head departments of elementary and secondary education. Their Innovation Lab Network is a group of states taking action to test and implement student-centered approaches to learning that will transform public education.

    http://www.ccsso.org/What_We_Do/Innovation_Lab_Net-
    work.html#sthash.abW0NRhI.dpuf

Early Learning Foundation offers training and support for school districts and parent organizations regarding competency based learning in the preschool to grade three years. Its Early Learning Success Initiative manages use of the *Essential Skill Inventories*, a competency based framework for measuring on-going progress toward essential skills in all the domains of early childhood.

    http://earlylearningfoundation.com/

International Association for K-12 Online Learning (iNACOL) supports the development and use of online, blended, and competency based learning models to achieve personalized and competency based learning, and offers a variety of reports and webinars.

http://www.inacol.org/

Jobs for the Future. JFF works with public and private partners across the country to design and expand models that: build basic skills, improve high school instruction, increase graduation rates, increase college entry, and provide support to help college students and job trainees.

http://www.jff.org/publications

KnowledgeWorks is a social enterprise focused on ensuring that students experience meaningful personalized learning, which supports success in college, career, and civic life.

http://www.knowledgeworks.org/

Lumina Foundation for Education is a private, Indianapolis-based foundation. Its mission is to expand student access to and success in education beyond high school. It has sponsored a series of reports on competency based higher education.

http://www.luminafoundation.org/resources

http://www.luminafoundation.org/files/resources/
competency-based-education-landscape.pdf

National Assessment of Educational Progress is the largest continuing and nationally representative assessment of what American students know and can do in core subjects. NAEP is a congressionally mandated project administered by the National Center for Education Statistics (NCES), within the Institute of Education Sciences (IES) of the US Department of Education.

http://nces.ed.gov/nationsreportcard/

National Association of Elementary School Principals is a professional organization serving elementary and middle school principals and other education leaders throughout the United States, Canada, and overseas. It has developed a competency framework for effective principals working with the early childhood years: *Leading Pre-K-3 Learning Communities: Competencies for Effective Principal Practice.*

>   https://www.naesp.org/sites/default/files/leading-pre-k-3-learning-communities-executive-summary.pdf

National Center for Competency-Based Learning (NCCBL) is a New Hampshire based 501(c)(3) nonprofit charitable organization founded in 2013.

>   http://www.nccbl.org/aboutus.html

Nellie Mae Education Foundation works with schools in New England to implement the principles of student-centered learning that is personalized, engaging, and competency based. They offer a rich library of publications that support competency based learning options.

>   http://www.nmefoundation.org/resources

New Hampshire Department of Education has been a leader in state competency based learning initiatives. The NHDoE has established model Literacy, Mathematics, Science, Work-Study, and Arts competencies for high school graduation.

>   http://education.nh.gov/innovations/hs_redesign/competencies.htm
>   http://education.nh.gov/innovations/hs_redesign/

Organisation for Economic Co-operation and Development (OECD) is the sponsoring agency for the Programme for International Student Assessment (PISA). This triennial international survey evaluates education systems worldwide by testing the skills and knowledge of 15-year-old students. In 2012, around 510,000 students in 65 economies took part in the PISA 2012 assessment of reading, mathematics, and science, representing about 28 million 15-year-olds globally. PISA is an ongoing triennial survey, allowing countries participating in successive surveys to compare their students' performance over time and assess the impact of education policy decisions.

>   http://www.oecd.org/pisa/keyfindings/pisa-2012-results.htm
>   http://www.oecd.org/

Rand Corporation is a research organization, working with nations around the world on issues including security, health, education, sustainability, growth, and development. Rand Education's research projects include competency based education.
http://www.rand.org/education/projects/competency-based-education.html

Re-inventing Schools Coalition (RISC) is a division of Marzano Research. It was established by core members of the team at Chugach School District and offers training and support materials to school districts. The history of RISC is described in *Delivering on the Promise: The Education Revolution* by DeLorenzo, Battino, Schreiber, and Gaddy-Carrio.
http://www.reinventingschools.org/

Study Guide

Chapter 1: Looking Back, a Parent's Remembrance

1. Describe a learning experience in which you remember being fully engaged in the learning process, challenged but not overwhelmed.
2. Describe a learning experience in which you remember being frustrated and overwhelmed by the work or presentation.
3. Write a fable that describes the learning life of a disadvantaged student within a typical modern school.

Chapter 2: Informed Instruction Leads to Competency, Part One

1. Describe a situation in which you were careful to use informed instruction with your own child.
2. What are some of the professions that have relied upon competency based learning systems for many years? Explain why that happened.
3. What happens when the pace of instruction does not match the readiness level of a student?

Chapter 3: The Curriculum-Driven Model

1. During the late 19th and early 20th century, public school systems developed using a standard curriculum. Explain how standard delivery of instruction met the needs of society in the early 1900s but fails to meet the needs of modern learners.
2. What vestiges of Horace Mann and Frederick Winslow Taylor can be seen in recent iterations of federal and state education policy?

3. Why have successful modern businesses moved away from one-size-fits-all learning and "the one best way" model of management?

Chapter 4: Standardized Delivery of Instruction

1. In what way did the standard delivery of instruction lead to the sorting of successful and non-successful students?
2. How did society's needs for an informed and literate population in 1900 differ from the needs of today?
3. In what way has the pressure of standardized testing in the last few decades influenced our use of standardized delivery of content?

Chapter 5: Failing to Meet Society's Learning Needs

1. In what ways has being a successful learner, and developing the capacity for intrinsically motivated learning, never been more crucial for the financial and social future of our children?
2. Describe, in your opinion, some of the conspicuous failures caused by our continued use of the curriculum-driven model of instruction.
3. In what ways are disadvantaged students especially affected by the curriculum-driven instructional model?
4. Find three sources for data that accurately describe the learning outcomes of our students. Describe any important reports or summaries from each source.

Chapter 6: Making the Case for Change

1. In 1991, the SCANS report advised: *Parents must insist that their sons and daughters master this know-how and that their local schools teach it. Unless you do, your children are unlikely to earn a decent living. If your children cannot learn these skills by the time they leave high school, they face bleak prospects & dead-end work, interrupted only by periods of unemployment,*

with little chance to climb a career ladder. Using your own words, write an advisory for parents today.

2. How do today's graduation requirements of your own school district line up with the 1991 SCANS advisory for the competencies and foundation skills students need to succeed?

3. In what way has our over-reliance on a Cover Test Sort educational model impacted the opportunity for many citizens to realize the American Dream?

4. Find one source that provides a set of educational outcomes that you believe is a good description of the skills and knowledge needed for success in the modern workplace and world.

Chapter 7: Giving Up Unproductive Mental Models

1. Quantity of content, grading on the curve, and sorting good and poor students. Among these three, in your opinion, which idea has caused the greatest harm to students? Why?

2. Some parents just want to know that their child is doing better than other children. To this parent, how would you describe the need for competency based learning?

3. Fifty years ago, the United States was generally considered to have the best educated workforce in the world. How did we lose that advantage?

Chapter 8: When Coverage Is Enough

1. Why should experiencing the joy of learning, and choosing to become a lifelong learner, be high priority goals for the design of a learning system? Explain your thoughts in detail.

2. Respond to the following statement: *The desire to learn, to wonder, to imagine, to explore, and to be curious is such an important part of being human. But our high-pressure modern version of curriculum-driven schooling produces lousy*

testing outcomes and also sucks the joy out of teaching and learning.
3. Describe some of the coverage-based learning experiences that have been a blessing for you.
4. Describe some learning goals that include ideas or topics you would love to explore without achieving specific competencies.

Chapter 9: Personalized Learning and Competency

1. Describe a situation in which someone personalized instruction for you.
2. Describe a situation in which you personalized instruction for a child or student.
3. In what way do quality digital learning systems match instruction to the needs and readiness of students?
4. Describe a real situation in which a company uses personalized instruction to train employees in crucial tasks.
5. Respond to this statement by the Oregon Education Roundtable: *In a proficiency system, failure or poor performance may be part of the student's learning curve, but it is not an outcome.*

Chapter 10: Principles of Instruction Leading to Competency

1. Rewrite the *Principles of Instruction Leading to Competency* in your own words.
2. Why is understanding the instructional-level needs of each child an important condition for competency based learning?
3. Identifying a small set of crucial learning outcomes is different than making a list of all the content we hope to "cover" in a course of study. Explain the difference.
4. Is it fair to let some students have more time to learn the content?
5. Is it fair to let some students move on to more advanced content when they are ready?

Chapter 11: Teaching Differently

1. Describe some important teacher behaviors that suffer in a content-driven instruction system.
2. What professional development needs must be considered as we begin to develop competency based learning systems?
3. Should high school credits be given for learning that is accomplished on the job, at home, independently, or anywhere outside the school?
4. Should college credits be given for learning that is accomplished on the job, at home, independently, or anywhere else outside the structure of a course?
5. How might the role of the parents change in a competency based learning system?
6. Describe the characteristics of men and women who will thrive as teachers within a competency based learning model.

Chapter 12: Identifying Crucial Outcomes

1. A successful competency based learning experience starts with the identification of clear learning goals. Why?
2. Are the skills needed to earn a tech certificate, pilot's license, or professional medical license clear? Contrast this with the experience of taking most high school or college courses.
3. A third grade student is given a C on his report card. What specific information about his progress toward becoming a successful reader does this grade offer?
4. In what way do good coaches use clear learning goals?

Chapter 13: Planning Instruction to Meet Students' Needs

1. If you are teaching a child to throw and catch, but the child is struggling to successfully catch the small ball, what innovations might you consider?

2. A student is struggling to solve two-digit subtraction problems that require borrowing. Upon analysis, you find that he does not have full proficiency for recognizing number groups (to 10), or solving combination problems (to 20) using manipulatives. What do you do with this information?
3. In a digital math program, a student scores 78 percent correct on a review assessment. What does the digital program do with this information?
4. Describe a learning program you have used that carefully monitors your progress and adapts to meet your needs.
5. What do you see as the greatest innovation opportunities for thoughtful educators as we move toward competency based learning?

Chapter 14: Self-Regulation and Intrinsic Motivation

1. How has our recent history of content-driven instruction and high-stakes testing impacted the development of intrinsic motivation among our students?
2. Self-regulation begins with the development of self-calming, focusing, persisting, delaying gratification, and adjusting your emotional, physical, and attentional state to meet the needs of your situation. How does the capacity for self-regulation impact a student's opportunity for success in school?
3. What activities or routines at school support the development of self-regulation?
4. What activities or routines at home support the development of self-regulation?
5. How will intrinsic motivation impact a student's success within a competency based learning system?

Chapter 15: Building a Positive Environment for Learning

1. What contributes to a learning environment in which students may feel highly anxious or insecure?

2. What contributes to an environment in which educators may also feel high anxious or insecure?
3. Could self-regulation and social-emotional skills be developed using a competency based model? Explain.
4. Describe a classroom in which kids learn to be calm and focused and to work well with other.
5. Describe a school environment that prioritizes the development of self-regulation, intrinsic motivation, and social-emotional skills.

Chapter 16: Creating a Learning Organizational Culture

1. How would you describe the organizational culture of your school or district?
2. *For decades, state and district education officials have set the expectations for what should be taught, in what order, and at what age. In recent years, politicians and bureaucrats have further dictated when and how this content will be tested, how schools will be graded, and how teachers will be evaluated. We are in the strong arms of a top-down Taylorian approach to every aspect of managing public education.* Please respond.
3. Is your school or district ready for the professional learning demands of competency based system?
4. In what way could your school or district begin to prepare for the transition to competency based learning?

Chapter 17: Learning for Understanding and Application

1. Young children are wired to learn. They are curious, engaged, and alive to learning. How does the experience of school affect this condition for most children? Why?
2. For intrinsic motivation to learn, why is it vital that learning goals be clear?
3. For intrinsic motivation to learn, why is it vital that learning goals be attainable?
4. For intrinsic motivation to learn, why is it vital that learning goals be personally meaningful?

5. How could choice be included into a competency based learning system?

Chapter 18: Masters of the Trade: Game Designers

1. While playing your favorite digital game (if you have one), in what ways do the game designers keep you engaged?
2. How does differentiated instruction at school use some of the learning concepts and principles demonstrated in high-quality digital games?
3. How does blended instruction at school use some of the learning concepts and principles demonstrated in high-quality digital games?
4. How does project-based instruction at school use some of the learning concepts and principles demonstrated in high-quality digital games?
5. Why don't game designers give grades to a player after each session?
6. How effectively do typical schools help a student develop an identity as a successful learner?

Chapter 19: State Competency Based Learning Initiatives

1. Research one state's competency initiative. What motivated the initiative? What were the first few steps in the process? What were the challenges they encountered?
2. States are approaching competency in many different ways. What factors are likely to influence the development of a competency based learning initiative in your state?
3. What are the challenges to consider when creating a definition of skills and knowledge needed for college and career readiness?
4. Are credit requirements for high school and college graduation an antiquated notion that no longer serves any purpose?

5. Should all students meet the exact same standards for high school graduation, or could personalized learning programs lead to different sets of meaningful skills?
6. How might competency based learning systems be applied to the early childhood years to improve learning outcomes for disadvantaged students?

Chapter 20: Competency Based Learning in Post-Secondary Education

1. Identify one competency based learning model for higher education within your state. Why was this developed, and how effectively do they ensure quality learning outcomes?
2. Why have medical and technical training programs long relied upon a competency based model?
3. Describe procedures for a primarily online IHE that would allow it to achieve level 5 status as a competency based learning system.
4. What are some of the challenges to a university considering moving toward competency based learning?
5. How could a professional education association contribute to the development of competency based learning systems for their members?
6. Choose one online university or training program, and evaluate its system using the rubric for considering the quality of an IHE competency based learning initiative.

Chapter 21: Competency Based Learning in Secondary Schools

1. In your opinion, is the use of Carnegie Units and credits for high school graduation an antiquated notion whose time has passed? Explain.
2. How do the intended purposes of the *European Framework of Key Competences for Lifelong Learning* (2007) contrast to

the intended purposes of the Common Core State Standards (2010).

3. What are the challenges to establishing state competency standards for high school graduation?
4. Imagine a high school that operates on a competency standards framework and has abandoned the credit requirement system. How would it function differently than typical high schools today?
5. In your district or community, what are the crucial outcomes that will help young men and women become ready to live and work in our changing world?

Chapter 22: Competency Based Learning in Elementary and Preschools

1. Why do third grade learning skills serve as such an important predictor of long-term learning success?
2. Is it possible to establish competency standards for language, phonologic skills, literacy, numeracy, motor skills, social-emotional skills, and self-regulation skills in the early learning years? What are the challenges?
3. How can parents participate in an early childhood competency based learning initiative?
4. Describe the relationship between formative and summative assessment in a successful, early learning CBL initiative.
5. In your view, could digital learning systems ever replace interactive physical and social learning during the early childhood years?

Chapter 23: Teacher Education: Building Pathways to Skills That Matter

1. How well did the teacher education or administrative education you experienced match the expectations of a high-quality competency based learning system?

2. What do you really think about the efficacy of the CEU system in your state?
3. Review one set of recommendations for teaching or administrative competency. Summarize and evaluate.
4. Develop a set of recommendations for teaching competency. These competencies could apply to a single discipline at one grade level, or to a level of instruction (early childhood, upper elementary, middle school, high school), or to any other segment of teaching. What are the specific skills that would allow teachers to demonstrate a high standard of competency?
5. Teacher competency matters. Explain.

Chapter 24: Distracted by the Debate over What to Cover

1. Do the Common Core State Standards represent one more attempt to describe the "one best way" of one-size-fits-all instruction? Explain.
2. In what ways has the introduction of CCSS and national testing systems impacted the lives of children in your school or your life as a teacher?
3. Describe three topics for professional learning you would love to see vigorously pursued in your school or district. What has prevented this professional learning from being considered in recent years?

Chapter 25: Defending Curriculum-Driven Instruction

1. Among the teachers and administrators you know well, what factors are likely to make the change to competency based learning difficult?
2. Describe a teacher you know who has used a similar course curriculum and/or set of lesson plans for many years. How will this teacher respond to the proposal to transition to a competency based learning system?
3. Is anyone in your district or institution of learning already using a competency based learning structure? If so, please describe.

Chapter 26: Transitioning from Curriculum-Driven to Competency Based Learning

1. In your schools, what is the point of beginning you would choose for competency based learning?
2. Who are the thinkers and leaders who will join you in the process of transforming toward competency based learning?
3. Describe one of the essential early steps in your transition plan and how you can support that step.

Chapter 27: Informed Instruction Leads to Competency, Part Two

1. Compare and contrast the underlying premises of the curriculum-driven instructional model with competency based learning.
2. What is your definition of informed instruction?
3. Describe your personal connection to the work of building competency based learning systems.

Chapter 28: Conclusion: The Spirit of Transformation

1. *Those of us who are educators, parents, and community leaders have the information, tools, and opportunity to create an educational process that works for many more students, a process that respects diversity, embraces personalization, and continuously improves.* Please respond.
2. What role will you choose in the transformation to competency based learning?

References

ACT (2013). *The Reality of College Readiness*. http://www.act.org/
readinessreality/13/pdf/Reality-of-College-Readiness-2013.pdf

Alberta Education (2011). *Framework for Student Learning: Competencies for Engaged Thinkers and Ethical Citizens with an Entrepreneurial Spirit*. http://education.alberta.ca/media/6581166/framework.pdf

Ames, C. (1992). Classrooms: Goals, Structures, and Student Motivation. *Journal of Educational Psychology, 84*, 261–271.

Annie E. Casey Foundation (2010). *Early Warning! Why Reading by the End of Third Grade Matters*. Baltimore, MD.

Annie E. Casey Foundation (2014). *Why Inequality Hurts Kids and Families*. http://www.aecf.org/blog/why-inequality-hurts-kids-and-families/

Betts, E. A. (1946). *Foundations of Reading Instruction with Emphasis on Differentiated Guidance*. New York, NY: American Book Company.

Bloomberg (2012). *Companies Say 3 Million Unfilled Positions in Skill Crisis: Jobs*. http://www.bloomberg.com/news/2012-07-25/companies-say-3-million-unfilled-positions-in-skill-crisis-jobs.html

British Columbia Ministry of Education (2013). *Exploring Curriculum Design, Transforming Curriculum and Assessment*. https://www.bced.gov.bc.ca/irp/docs/exp_curr_design.pdf

British Columbia Ministry of Education update (2015). *British Columbia Education Plan*. http://www.bcedplan.ca/

Burns, M. K. (2007). Reading at the Instructional Level with Children Identified as Learning Disabled: Potential Implications for Response to Intervention. *School Psychology Quarterly, 22*, 297–313.

Buros Center for Testing (1990). *Standards for Teacher Competence in Educational Assessment of Students*. http://buros.org/standards-teacher-competence-educational-assessment-students

Colorado Dept. of Education (2013). *Colorado's Graduation Guidelines: 2013 & Beyond.* http://www.cde.state.co.us/postsecondary/ graduationguidelinesworkgroupwebinar

Council of Chief State School Officers (CCSSO, 2015). *Innovation in Action: State Pathways for Advancing Student Centered Learning.* http://www.ccsso.org/Documents/ILN%20Logic%20Model%20 White%20Paper-online%20file.pdf

Council of Chief State School Officers (CCSSO) Interstate Teacher Assessment and Support Consortium (2013). *Model Core Teaching Standards and Learning Progressions for Teachers 1.0.* http://www.ccsso.org/Resources/Publications/InTASC_Model_ Core_Teaching_Standards_2011_MS_Word_Version.html

Csikszentmihalyi, M. (1985). Emergent Motivation and the Evolution of the Self. In D. A. Kleiber & M. Maehr (Eds.), *Advances in Motivation and Achievement,* (Vol. 4, pp. 93–119). Greenwich, CT: JAI Press.

DeLorenzo, R., Battino, W., Schreiber, R., & Gaddy-Carrio, B. (2008). *Delivering on the Promise.* Bloomington, IN: Solution Tree.

Dempster, F. N. (1993). Exposing Our Students to Less Should Help Them Learn. *Phi Delta Kappan, 74*(6), 432–437.

Downs, R. B. (1974). *Horace Mann: Champion of the Public Schools.* New York: Twayne Publishers.

Driscoll, M. P. (1994). *Psychology of Learning for Instruction.* Boston, MA: Allyn & Bacon Publishers.

Duckworth, A. L., Peterson, C., Matthews, M. D., & Kelly, D. R. (2007). Grit: Perseverance and Passion for Long-Term Goals. *Journal of Personality and Social Psychology, 92*(6), 1087–1101. http://dx.doi. org/10.1037/0022–3514.92.6.1087

DuFour, R., & Eaker, R. (1998). *Professional Learning Communities at Work: Best Practices for Enhancing Student Achievement.* Bloomington, IN: Solution Tree.

DuFour, R., Eaker, R., & DuFour, R. (2008). *Revisiting Professional Learning Communities at Work: New Insights for Improving Schools.* Bloomington, IN: Solution Tree.

Educational Testing Service (ETS) (2015). *America's Skills Challenge: Millennials and the Future.* OECD Programme for International Assessment of Adult Competencies.

EPE Research Center (2010). *The Nation's Long and Winding Path to Graduation*. http://www.edweek.org/media/34gradrate-c1.pdf.

European Commission (2007). *Key Competences for Lifelong Learning: European Reference Framework*. Luxembourg: Office for Official Publications of the European Communities. http://eur-lex.europa.eu/LexUriServ/LexUriServ.do?uri=OJ:L:2006:394:0010:0018:EN:PDF

Fielding, L., Kerr, N., & Rosier, P. (2007). *Annual Growth for All Students, Catch Up Growth for Those Who Are Behind*. Kennewick, WA: The New Foundation Press.

Forbes (2012). *60% of College Grads Can't Find Work in Their Field. Is a Management Degree the Answer?* http://www.forbes.com/sites/jamesmarshallcrotty/2012/03/01/most-college-grads-cant-find-work-in-their-field-is-a-management-degree-the-answer/

Fortune (2014). *Wealth Inequality in America: It's Worse Than You Think*. http://fortune.com/2014/10/31/inequality-wealth-income-us/

Fuchs, L., & Fuchs, D. (1988). Curriculum-Based Measurement: A Methodology for Evaluating and Improving Student Programs. *Assessment for Effective Intervention, 14*(1), 3–13.

Fullan, M., & Hargreaves, A. (1996). *What's Worth Fighting for in Your School?* New York, NY: Teachers College Press.

Gickling, E. E., & Armstrong, D. L. (1978). Levels of Instructional Difficulty as Related to On-Task Behavior, Task Completion, and Comprehension. *Journal of Learning Disabilities, 11*, 32–39.

Hattie, J. (2009). *Visible Learning*. London: Routledge.

Hernandez, D. (2011). *Double Jeopardy: How Third-Grade Reading Skills and Poverty Influence High School Graduation*. Baltimore, MD: Annie E. Casey Foundation. http://www.cde.state.co.us/SecondaryInitiatives/GraduationGuidelin es.htm

International Association for K-12 Online Learning (2014). *iNACOL Blended Learning Teacher Competency Framework*. https://www.inacol.org/wp-content/uploads/2014/10/iNACOL-Blende d-Learning-Teacher-Competency-Framework.pdf

Kanigel, R. (1997). *The One Best Way: Frederick Winslow Taylor and the Enigma of Efficiency*. New York, NY: Viking.

Laitinen, A. (2012). *Cracking the Credit Hour, New America Foundation*. https://www.newamerica.org/education-policy/cracking-the-credit-hour/

Lepper, M. R., & Hodell, M. (1989). Intrinsic Motivation in the Classroom. In C. Ames & R. Ames (Eds.), *Research on Motivation in Education* (Vol. 3, pp. 73–105). San Diego, CA: Academic Press.

Maine Department of Education (2012). *Education Evolving: Maine's Plan for Putting Learners First*. http://maine.gov/doe/plan

Marzano, R. J. (2003). *What Works in Schools: Translating Research into Action*. Alexandria, VA: Association for Supervision and Curriculum Development.

Mayer, R. (2002). Rote Versus Meaningful Learning. *Theory Into Practice, 41*(4), 226.

MetLife Survey of the American Teacher: Challenges for School Leadership. (2013). New York, NY: Metropolitan Life Insurance Company.

Mischel, W., Shoda, Y., & Rodriguez, M. (1989). Delay of Gratification in Children. *Science, 244*, 933–938.

Mission Readiness (2009). *Ready Willing and Unable to Serve*, a Report Prepared for the Joint Chiefs of Staff. http://cdn.missionreadiness.org/NATEE1109.pdf

Moffitt, T., Arseneault, L., Belsky, D., Dickson, N., Hancox, R., Harrington, H., Houts, R., Poulton, R., Roberts, B., Ross, S., Sears, M., Thomson, W., & Caspi, A. (2011). A Gradient of Childhood Self-Control Predicts Health, Wealth, and Public Safety. *Proceedings of the National Academy of Sciences of the United States of America, 108*(7), 2693–2698. http://www.ncbi.nlm.nih.gov/pmc/articles/PMC3041102/

National Assessment of Educational Progress (2013). *The Nation's Report Card*. http://nationsreportcard.gov/reading_math_g12_2013/#/

National Association of Elementary School Principals (2014). *Leading Pre-K-3 Learning Communities: Competencies for Effective Principal Practice*. https://www.naesp.org/sites/default/files/leading-pre-k-3-learning-communities-executive-summary.pdf

National Center for Education Statistics (2014). U.S. Department of Education, Common Core of Data (CCD), "NCES Common Core of Data State Dropout and Graduation Rate Data file," School Year 2010–11, Provisional Version 1a.

National Center for Education Statistics (2015a). *National Assessment of Educational Progress*. http://nces.ed.gov/nationsreportcard/

National Center for Education Statistics (2015). Table 221.85. Average National Assessment of Educational Progress (NAEP) reading scale score, by age and selected student characteristics: Selected years, 1971 through 2012. https://nces.ed.gov/programs/digest/d13/tables/dt13_221.85.asp

National Center for Education Statistics (2015). Table 222.85. Average National Assessment of Educational Progress (NAEP) mathematics scale score, by age and selected student characteristics: Selected years, 1973 through 2012. https://nces.ed.gov/programs/digest/d13/tables/dt13_222.85.asp

National Mathematics Advisory Council (2008). *Foundations for Success: The Final Report of the National Mathematics Advisory Council*. Washington D.C., US Department of Education.

National Technical Information Service (1991). Secretary's Commission on Achieving Necessary Skills (SCANS), U.S. Department of Commerce, NTIS Order Number: PB92–146711INZ.

New Hampshire DOE (2007). *New Hampshire's Vision for Redesign, Moving from High Schools to Learning Communities*. http://education.nh.gov/innovations/hs_redesign/documents/vision.pdf

New Hampshire DOE (2014). *Minimum Standards for Public School Approval*. http://education.nh.gov/legislation/documents/ed3062014-min-stands.pdf

New Hampshire K-12 Science Competencies (2014). *New Hampshire State Board of Education*. http://education.nh.gov/innovations/hs_redesign/documents/ccrs-competencies-science.pdf

OECD (2011). *Divided We Stand: Why Inequality Keeps Rising, Organisation for Economic Co-operation and Development*. http://www.oecd.org/els/soc/49499779.pdf

OECD (2012). *Programme for International Student Assessment*. http://www.oecd.org/pisa/

Oregon Education Roundtable (2009). *Proficiency Based Learning*. http://theworldlink.com/news/local/education/oregon-education-roundtable—-proficiency-based-instruction-and-assessment/pdf_35e52372–2d1a-11e3-bdc3–001a4bcf887a.html

Professional Learning Communities: *Four Essential Questions and How We Respond*. (2014). Stevenson Elementary School. http://www.dps61.org/domain/1578

Schmidt, W. H., & Cogan, L. S. (2009). The Myth of Equal Content. *Educational Leadership 3*(3), 44–47. Alexandria, VA: ASCD.

Schmidt, W. H., McKnight, C. C., & Raizen, S. A. (1996). *Splintered Vision: An Investigation of U.S. Science and Mathematics Education: Executive Summary*. Lansing, MI: U.S. National Research Center for the Third International Mathematics and Science Study, Michigan State University.

Schmidt, W. H., McKnight, C. C., Houang, R. T., Wang, H. C., Wiley, D. E., Cogan, L. S., & Wolfe, R. G. (2001). *Why Schools Matter: A Cross-National Comparison of Curriculum and Learning*. San Francisco, CA: Jossey-Bass.

Schmidt, W. H., Wang, H. A., & McKnight, C. C. (2005). Curriculum Coherence: An Examination of U.S. Mathematics and Science Content Standards from an International Perspective. *Journal of Curriculum Studies, 37*(5), 525–529.

Schmoker, M., & Marzano, R. (1999). Realizing the Promise of Standards-Based Education. *Education Leadership, 56*(6), 17–21.

Snow, C. E., Burns, S., & Griffin, P. (Eds.) (1998). *Preventing Reading Difficulties in Young Children, Report of the Committee on the Prevention of Reading Difficulties in Young Children*. Washington, DC: National Academy Press.

Sornson, B. (2012a). *Essential Skills Inventories, Preschool through Grade 3*. Brighton, MI: Early Learning Foundation.

Sornson, B. (2012b). *Fanatically Formative: Successful Learning during the Crucial K–3 Years*. Thousand Oaks, CA: Corwin Press.

Sornson, B. (2014). *Essential Math Skills*. Huntington Beach, CA: Shell Education.

Sornson, B. (2015). The Effects of Using the Essential Skills Inventory on Teacher Perception of High-Quality Classroom Instruction. *Preventing School Failure: Alternative Education for Children and Youth, 59*(3), 161–167.

Sornson, B., & Davis, D. (2013). Focus on Essential Learning Outcomes. *Journal of Research Initiatives, 1*(1), Article 8. http://digitalcommons.uncfsu.edu/jri/vol1/iss1/8

State of Vermont Board of Education (2013). *Vermont Education Quality Standards.* http://education.vermont.gov/documents/ EDU_EQS_01_23_14_Proposed_Final_Rule.pdf

Stiggins, R. (1999). Assessment, Student Confidence, and School Success. *Phi Delta Kappan, 81*(3), 191.

Sturgis, C. (2014). *Progress and Proficiency, Redesigning Grading for Competency Education, Competency Works Issue Brief.* http://www. competencyworks.org/wp-content/uploads/2014/01/ CW-Progress-and-Proficiency-January-2014.pdf

Taylor, B. P. (2010). *Horace Mann's Troubling Legacy: The Education of Democratic Citizens.* Lawrence, KA: University Press of Kansas.

Taylor, F. (1911). *The Principles of Scientific Management.* New York and London: Harper & Brothers.

Teacher Leadership Consortium (2014). *Teacher Leader Model Standards.* https://www.ets.org/s/education_topics/teaching_ quality/pdf/teacher_leader_model_standards.pdf

Torgesen, J.K. (1998). Catch Them Before They Fail. *American Educator, 22*(1–2), 32–39.

Torgesen, J. K. (2002). The Prevention of Reading Difficulties. *Journal of School Psychology, 40,* 7–26.

United Nations Educational, Scientific and Cultural Organization (2008). *ICT Competency Standards for Teachers, Implementation Guidelines.* http://unesdoc.unesco.org/images/0015/001562/ 156209E.pdf

US Census Bureau (2014a). *Educational Attainment in the United States: 2013.* Retrieved March 26, 2014.

US Census Bureau (2014b). *Historical Income Tables: Income Inequality.* http://www.census.gov/hhes/www/income/data/historical/ inequality/

US Department of Education (2010). *National Education Technology Plan.* http://tech.ed.gov/netp/

US Department of Labor (1991). *What Work Requires of Schools: A SCANS Report for America 2000.* Secretary's Commission on Achieving Necessary Skills.

Vygotsky, L. S. (1978). *Mind in Society: The Development of Higher Psychological Processes.* Cambridge, MA: Harvard University Press.